MW00603535

What Readers Are Saying About
Metaprogramming Ruby 2

This is the one book about Ruby that makes you go "So *that's* how it works" over and over again, as concepts such as the object model, DSLs, and blocks fall into place with that satisfying "Click!" sound. It's a great guide to what happens under the hood of a language that seems to involve a kind of magic deep inside. I highly recommend it.

➤ **Peter Bakhirev**
Lead software engineer, Gilt City

The previous edition of *Metaprogramming Ruby* changed my life and my code, and helped me get my first programming job. You would think there would be no way to improve on a book that good, but Paolo Perrotta has done it. Learn to unlock the hidden potential of this beautiful language, and fall in love with Ruby again.

➤ **Richard Schneeman**
Programmer, Heroku

For gem authors and application developers alike, this book lays down the foundation everyone needs to harness the full power of Ruby. Paolo describes metaprogramming in a fun and approachable way for all skill levels. The knowledge garnered from reading this book will help you write cleaner code and work more effectively with legacy codebases.

➤ **Paul Elliott**
Rocketeer, Hashrocket

If you want to follow the path of Ruby metaprogramming mastery, then this book is the best companion you can think of, no matter what your level is. I had struggled with Ruby metaprogramming for years until I read this book; now it all makes sense.

➤ **Fabien Catteau**
  Software developer, Tech-Angels

This is a book that everyone who wants to have a deeper understanding of the inner workings of Ruby and Ruby on Rails should read. The "spells" described in this book are invaluable tools to understand and use Ruby to its full extent. This is not only about metaprogramming, but also about taking your Ruby programming to a different level.

➤ **Kosmas Chatzimichalis**
  Software engineer

I'm a huge Python fan, so I was supposed to disregard Ruby. Paolo made me appreciate it. Not only is *Metaprogramming Ruby* the book that allowed me to wrap my head around this esoteric and fascinating topic, but it also made me rethink the way I write code in other languages.

➤ **Arialdo Martini**
  Programmer, JobRapido.com

This book uncovers all the ins and outs of the art of metaprogramming in Ruby, with a no-nonsense approach and an irony that transpires from vibrant prose, never boring, without compromising any of its insightfulness. *Metaprogramming Ruby* is one of those books that any serious Rubyist (and even the pros) will want to revisit from time to time.

➤ **Piergiuliano Bossi**
   Principal engineer lead, Points

Metaprogramming Ruby has been a hugely influential book for me, especially during a time when I wanted to learn about the inner workings of Ruby. Paolo "Nusco" Perrotta made what is normally a complex topic fun, enjoyable, and very approachable.

➤ **Josh Kalderimis**
   CEO, Travis CI

Metaprogramming Ruby 2
Program Like the Ruby Pros

Paolo Perrotta

The Pragmatic Bookshelf

Raleigh, North Carolina

Many of the designations used by manufacturers and sellers to distinguish their products are claimed as trademarks. Where those designations appear in this book, and The Pragmatic Programmers, LLC was aware of a trademark claim, the designations have been printed in initial capital letters or in all capitals. The Pragmatic Starter Kit, The Pragmatic Programmer, Pragmatic Programming, Pragmatic Bookshelf, PragProg and the linking *g* device are trademarks of The Pragmatic Programmers, LLC.

Every precaution was taken in the preparation of this book. However, the publisher assumes no responsibility for errors or omissions, or for damages that may result from the use of information (including program listings) contained herein.

Our Pragmatic books, screencasts, and audio books can help you and your team create better software and have more fun. Visit us at *https://pragprog.com*.

The team that produced this book includes:

Lynn Beighley (editor)
Potomac Indexing, LLC (index)
Cathleen Small (copyedit)
Dave Thomas (layout)
Janet Furlow (producer)
Ellie Callahan (support)

For sales, volume licensing, and support, please contact *support@pragprog.com*.

For international rights, please contact *rights@pragprog.com*.

Copyright © 2014 The Pragmatic Programmers, LLC.
All rights reserved.

No part of this publication may be reproduced, stored in a retrieval system, or transmitted, in any form, or by any means, electronic, mechanical, photocopying, recording, or otherwise, without the prior consent of the publisher.

Printed in the United States of America.
ISBN-13: 978-1-94122-212-6
Printed on acid-free paper.
Book version: P3.0—June 2016

I was thirteen, and I was tired of hanging out at the local toy shop to play Intellivision games. I wanted my own videogame console. I'd been bugging my parents for a while, with no success.

Then I found an alternative: I could play games on a computer as well. So I asked my parents to buy me one of those new 8-bit computers—you know, to learn useful stuff. My dad agreed, and my mom took me to the shop and bought me a Sinclair ZX Spectrum.

Mom, Dad... Here is something that I should've told you more often in my life: thank you. This book is dedicated to the two of you. I'm hoping it will make you proud, just like your once-kid is proud of you. And while I'm here, I have something to confess about that life-changing day thirty years ago: I didn't really want to learn stuff. I just wanted to play.

In fact, that's what I've been doing all these years.

Contents

Part I — Metaprogramming Ruby

Part II — Metaprogramming in Rails

Part III — Appendixes

Foreword

Ruby inherits characteristics from various languages—Lisp, Smalltalk, C, and Perl, to name a few. Metaprogramming comes from Lisp (and Smalltalk). It's a bit like magic, which makes something astonishing possible. There are two kinds of magic: white magic, which does good things, and black magic, which can do nasty things. Likewise, there are two aspects to metaprogramming. If you discipline yourself, you can do good things, such as enhancing the language without tweaking its syntax by macros or enabling internal domain-specific languages. But you can fall into the dark side of metaprogramming. Metaprogramming can confuse easily.

Ruby trusts you. Ruby treats you as a grown-up programmer. It gives you great power, such as metaprogramming. But you need to remember that with great power comes great responsibility.

Enjoy programming in Ruby.

matz

Acknowledgments

Thank you, Joe Armstrong, Satoshi Asakawa, Peter Bakhirev, Paul Barry, Juanjo Bazán, Emmanuel Bernard, Roberto Bettazzoni, Ola Bini, Piergiuliano Bossi, Simone Busoli, Alessandro Campeis, Kosmas Chatzimichalis, Andrea Cisternino, Davide D'Alto, Pietro Di Bello, Mauro Di Nuzzo, Marco Di Timoteo, Paul Elliott, Eric Farkas, Mauricio Fernandez, Francisco Fernández Castaño, Jay Fields, Michele Finelli, Neal Ford, Florian Frank, Sanne Grinovero, Federico Gobbo, Florian Groß, Sebastian Hennebrüder, Doug Hudson, Jurek Husakowski, Lyle Johnson, Lisa Maria Jones, Josh Kalderimis, Murtuza Kutub, Marc Lainez, Daniele Manni, Luca Marchetti, Arialdo Martini, Kado Masanori, MenTaLguY, Nicola Moretto, Sandro Paganotti, Alessandro Patriarca, Carlo Pecchia, Susanna Perrotta, John Pignata, Andrea Provaglio, Mike Roberts, Martin Rodgers, 琳琳的小狗, Richard Schneeman, Bartlomiej Skwira, Joe Sims, Jeremy Sydik, Andrea Tomasini, Mauro Tortonesi, Marco Trincardi, Ivan Vaghi, Giancarlo Valente, Davide Varvello, Elzie Vergine.

Thank you, readers who gave feedback and reported errata. Thank you, contributors to the open-source code I show in this book.

Thank you, Jim Weirich. We owe you a lot.

Thank you, Pragmatic people: Ellie Callahan, Janet Furlow, Andy Hunt, David Kelly, Susannah Pfalzer, Cathleen Small, Dave Thomas, Devon Thomas. Thank you, Lynn Beighley, for smoothing out my prose and calling me back to duty when I drifted astray, like Jill Steinberg had done for the first edition.

It takes a long time to update a book. You turn back once the job is done, and you're surprised by how many things have changed in your life. On the other hand, some things haven't. Thank you, Ivana Gancheva, my precious friend.

Will write code that writes code that writes code for food.

➤ *Martin Rodgers*

Introduction

Metaprogramming...it sounds cool! It sounds like a design technique for high-level enterprise architects or a faddish buzzword that has found its way into press releases.

In fact, far from being an abstract concept or a bit of marketing-speak, metaprogramming is a collection of down-to-earth, pragmatic coding techniques. It doesn't just sound cool; it *is* cool. Here are some things you can do with metaprogramming in the Ruby language:

- Say you want to write a Ruby program that connects to an external system
  —maybe a web service or a Java program. With metaprogramming, you can write a wrapper that takes *any* method call and routes it to the external system. If somebody adds methods to the external system later, you don't have to change your Ruby wrapper; the wrapper will support the new methods right away. That's magic.

- Maybe you have a problem that would best be solved with a programming language that's specific to that problem. You could go to the trouble of writing your own language, custom parser and all. Or you could just use Ruby, bending its syntax until it looks like a specific language for your problem. You can even write your own little interpreter that reads code written in your Ruby-based language from a file.

- You can aggressively remove duplication from your Ruby code while keeping it elegant and clean. Imagine twenty methods in a class that all look the same. How about defining all those methods at once, with just a few lines of code? Or maybe you want to call a sequence of similarly named methods. How would you like a single short line of code that calls all the methods whose names match a pattern—like, say, all methods that begin with *test*?

- You can stretch and twist Ruby to meet your needs, rather than adapt to the language as it is. For example, you can enhance any class (even a core class like Array) with that method you miss so dearly, you can wrap logging functionality around a method that you want to monitor, you can execute custom code whenever a client inherits from your favorite class...the list goes on. You are limited only by your own, undoubtedly fertile, imagination.

Metaprogramming gives you the power to do all these things. Let's see how this book will help you learn about it.

About This Book

Part I, *Metaprogramming Ruby*, is the core of the book. Chapter 1, *The M Word*, on page 3, walks you through the basic idea behind metaprogramming. The following chapters tell the story of a week in the life of a newly hired Ruby programmer and his or her more experienced colleague:

- Ruby's object model is the land in which metaprogramming lives. Chapter 2, *Monday: The Object Model*, on page 11, provides a map to this land. This chapter introduces you to the most basic metaprogramming techniques. It also reveals the secrets behind Ruby classes and *method lookup*, the process by which Ruby finds and executes methods.

- Once you understand method lookup, you can do some fancy things with methods: you can create methods at runtime, intercept method calls, route calls to another object, or even accept calls to methods that don't exist. All these techniques are explained in Chapter 3, *Tuesday: Methods*, on page 45.

- Methods are members of a larger family also including entities such as blocks and lambdas. Chapter 4, *Wednesday: Blocks*, on page 73, is your field manual for everything related to these entities. It also presents an example of writing a *domain-specific language*, a powerful conceptual tool that Ruby coders tend to love. This chapter also comes with its own share of tricks, explaining how you can package code and execute it later or how you can carry variables across scopes.

- Speaking of scopes, Ruby has a special scope that deserves a close look: the scope of class definitions. Chapter 5, *Thursday: Class Definitions*, on page 105, talks about this scope and introduces you to some of the most powerful weapons in a metaprogrammer's arsenal. It also introduces *singleton classes*, the last concept you need to make sense of Ruby's most perplexing features.

- Finally, Chapter 6, *Friday: Code That Writes Code*, on page 139, puts it all together through an extended example that uses techniques from all the previous chapters. The chapter also rounds out your metaprogramming training with two new topics: the somewhat controversial eval method and the callback methods that you can use to intercept events in the object model.

Part II of the book, *Metaprogramming in Rails*, is a case study in metaprogramming. It contains short chapters that focus on different areas of Rails, the flagship Ruby framework. By looking at Rails' source code, you'll see how master Ruby coders use metaprogramming in the real world to develop great software, and you'll also understand how some metaprogramming techniques evolved in the last few years.

Three appendixes close the book. Appendix 1, *Common Idioms*, on page 217, is a grab-bag of common techniques that are not explained anywhere else in the book. Appendix 2, *Domain-Specific Languages*, on page 227, is a quick look at a programming approach that is common among Ruby developers. Appendix 3, *Spell Book*, on page 231, is a catalog of all the spells in the book, complete with code examples.

"Wait a minute," I can hear you saying. "What the heck are *spells*?" Oh, right, sorry. Let me explain.

Spells

This book contains a number of metaprogramming techniques that you can use in your own code. Some people might call these *patterns* or maybe *idioms*. Neither of these terms is very popular among Rubyists, so I'll call them *spells* instead. Even if there's nothing magical about them, they *do* look like magic spells to Ruby newcomers.

You'll find references to spells everywhere in the book. I reference a spell with the convention *Class Macro (117)* or *String of Code (141)*, for example. The number in parentheses is the page where the spell receives a name. If you need a quick reference to a spell, you'll find it in Appendix 3, *Spell Book*, on page 231.

Quizzes

Every now and then, this book also throws a quiz at you. You can skip these quizzes and just read the solution, but you'll probably want to solve them on your own just because they're fun.

Some quizzes are traditional coding exercises; others require you to get off your keyboard and think. All include a solution, but most quizzes have more than one possible answer. Please, feel free to go wild and experiment.

Notation Conventions

This book is chock full of code examples. To show you that a line of code results in a value, I print that value as a comment on the same line:

```
-1.abs          # => 1
```

If a code example is supposed to print a result rather than return it, I show that result after the code:

```
puts 'Testing... testing...'
```

❮ Testing... testing...

In most cases, the text uses the same code syntax that Ruby uses: MyClass.my_method is a class method, MyClass::MY_CONSTANT is a constant defined within a class, and so on. There are a couple of exceptions to this rule. First, I identify instance methods with the *hash* notation, like the Ruby documentation does (MyClass#my_method). This is useful to distinguish class methods and instance methods. Second, I use a hash prefix to identify singleton classes (#MySingletonClass).

Ruby has a flexible syntax, so few universal rules exist for things like indentation and the use of parentheses. Programmers tend to adopt the syntax that they find most readable in each specific case. In this book, I try to follow the most common conventions. For example, I skip parentheses when I call a method without parameters (as in my_string.reverse), but I tend to use parentheses when I pass parameters (as in my_string.gsub("x", "y")).

Some of the code in this book comes straight from existing open-source libraries. Some of these are standard Ruby libraries, so you should already have them. You can install the others with the gem command. For example, if I show you a piece of code from Builder 3.2.2, and you want to install the entire library to explore its source by yourself, then you can use gem install builder -v 3.2.2. Be aware of the version, because the code might have changed in more recent versions of Builder.

To avoid clutter (and make the code easier to understand in isolation), I'll sometimes take the liberty of editing the original code slightly. However, I'll do my best to keep the spirit of the original source intact.

Unit Tests

This book follows two developers as they go about their day-to-day work. As the story unfolds, you may notice that these two characters rarely write tests. Does this book condone untested code?

Please rest assured that it doesn't. In fact, the original draft of this book included unit tests for all code examples. In the end, I found that those tests distracted from the metaprogramming techniques that are the meat of the book, so the tests fell on the cutting-room floor. This doesn't mean you shouldn't write tests for your own metaprogramming endeavors.

On those occasions where I did show test code in this book, I used Ruby's test-unit library. Most versions of Ruby come with this library already installed. If yours didn't, you can install it with gem install test-unit.

Ruby Versions

Ruby is continuously changing and improving. However, this very fluidity can be problematic when you try a piece of code on the latest version of the language, only to find that it doesn't work anymore. This is not overly common, but it can happen with metaprogramming, which pushes Ruby to its limits.

This book is written for Ruby 2. As I write, Ruby 2.2 is the most recent stable version of the language, and it's mostly compatible with Ruby 2.0. Some people still run older versions of Ruby, which miss a few important features from 2.x—notably, Refinements and Module#prepend. In the text, I'll refer to Ruby 2.2, and I'll tell you which features were introduced either in Ruby 2.1 or in Ruby 2.0.

When I talk about Ruby versions, I'm talking about the "official" interpreter (sometimes called MRI for *Matz's Ruby Interpreter*[1]). There are many alternate Ruby implementations. Two of the most popular ones are JRuby, which runs on the Java Virtual Machine,[2] and Rubinius.[3] Alternate implementations usually take a few versions to catch up with MRI — so if you use one of them, be aware that some of the examples in this book might not yet work on your interpreter.

Book Editions

The first edition of this book focused on Ruby 1.8, which has since been deprecated. I updated the text to reflect the new features in Ruby, especially the ones that have been introduced by Ruby 2.x.

The chapters in Part II use the Rails source code as a source of examples. Rails has changed a lot since the first edition, so these chapters are almost a complete rewrite of the first edition's content.

---

1. http://www.ruby-lang.org
2. http://jruby.codehaus.org
3. http://rubini.us/

Apart from the changes in the language and the libraries, some of my personal opinions also changed since the first edition of this book. I learned to be wary of some techniques, such as *Ghost Methods (57)*, and fonder of others, such as *Dynamic Methods (51)*. Parts of the new text reflect these changes of heart.

Finally, this second edition is a general cleanup of the first edition's text. I updated many examples that were using gems and source code that have been forgotten or changed since the previous book; I added a few spells and removed a few others that don't seem very relevant anymore; I toned down the "story" in the text when it was adding too many words to long technical explanations; and I went through every sentence again, fixing things that needed fixing and addressing errata and suggestions from the readers. Whether you're a new reader or a fan of the first edition, I hope you like the result.

About You

Most people consider metaprogramming an advanced topic. To play with the constructs of a Ruby program, you have to know how these constructs work in the first place. How do you know whether you're enough of an "advanced" Rubyist to deal with metaprogramming? Well, if you can understand the code in the very first chapter without much trouble, then you are well equipped to move forward.

If you're not confident about your skills, you can take a simple self-test. Which kind of code would you write to iterate over an array? If you thought about the each method, then you know enough Ruby to follow the ensuing text. If you thought about the for keyword, then you're probably new to Ruby. In the second case, you can still embark on this metaprogramming adventure—just take an introductory Ruby text along with you, or take the excellent interactive tutorial at the *Try Ruby!* site.[4]

Are you on board, then? Great! Let's start.

---

4.   http://tryruby.org

Part I

Metaprogramming Ruby

## CHAPTER 1

The M Word

Metaprogramming is writing code that writes code.

We'll get to a more precise definition soon, but this one will do for now. What do I mean by "code that writes code," and how is that useful in your daily work? Before I answer those questions, let's take a step back and look at programming languages themselves.

Ghost Towns and Marketplaces

Think of your source code as a world teeming with vibrant citizens: variables, classes, methods, and so on. If you want to get technical, you can call these citizens *language constructs*.

In many programming languages, language constructs behave more like ghosts than fleshed-out citizens: you can see them in your source code, but they disappear before the program runs. Take C++, for example. Once the compiler has finished its job, things like *variables* and *methods* have lost their concreteness; they are just locations in memory. You can't ask a class for its instance methods, because by the time you ask the question, the class has faded away. In languages such as C++, runtime is an eerily quiet place—a ghost town.

In other languages, such as Ruby, runtime is more like a busy marketplace. Most language constructs are still there, buzzing all around. You can even walk up to a language construct and ask it questions about itself. This is called *introspection*.

Let's watch introspection in action. Take a look at the following code.

```
the_m_word/introspection.rb
class Greeting
  def initialize(text)
    @text = text
  end

  def welcome
    @text
  end
end

my_object = Greeting.new("Hello")
```

I defined a Greeting class and created a Greeting object. I can now turn to the language constructs and ask them questions.

```
my_object.class                              # => Greeting
```

I asked my_object about its class, and it replied in no uncertain terms: "I'm a Greeting." Now I can ask the class for a list of its instance methods.

```
my_object.class.instance_methods(false)      # => [:welcome]
```

The class answered with an array containing a single method name: welcome. (The false argument means, "List only instance methods you defined yourself, not those ones you inherited.") Let's peek into the object itself, asking for its instance variables.

```
my_object.instance_variables                 # => [:@text]
```

Again, the object's reply was loud and clear. Because objects and classes are first-class citizens in Ruby, you can get a lot of information from running code.

However, this is only half of the picture. Sure, you can read language constructs at runtime, but what about *writing* them? What if you want to add new instance methods to Greeting, alongside welcome, while the program is running? You might be wondering why on earth anyone would want to do that. Allow me to explain by telling a story.

The Story of Bob, Metaprogrammer

Bob, a newcomer to Ruby, has a grand plan: he'll write the biggest Internet social network ever for movie buffs. To do that, he needs a database of movies and movie reviews. Bob makes it a practice to write reusable code, so he decides to build a simple library to persist objects in the database.

Bob's First Attempt

Bob's library maps each class to a database table and each object to a record. When Bob creates an object or accesses its attributes, the object generates a string of SQL and sends it to the database. All this functionality is wrapped in a class:

`the_m_word/orm.rb`

```ruby
class Entity
  attr_reader :table, :ident

  def initialize(table, ident)
    @table = table
    @ident = ident
    Database.sql "INSERT INTO #{@table} (id) VALUES (#{@ident})"
  end

  def set(col, val)
    Database.sql "UPDATE #{@table} SET #{col}='#{val}' WHERE id=#{@ident}"
  end

  def get(col)
    Database.sql ("SELECT #{col} FROM #{@table} WHERE id=#{@ident}")[0][0]
  end
end
```

In Bob's database, each table has an id column. Each Entity stores the content of this column and the name of the table to which it refers. When Bob creates an Entity, the Entity saves itself to the database. Entity#set generates SQL that updates the value of a column, and Entity#get generates SQL that returns the value of a column. (In case you care, Bob's Database class returns recordsets as arrays of arrays.)

Bob can now subclass Entity to map to a specific table. For example, class Movie maps to a database table named movies:

```ruby
class Movie < Entity
  def initialize(ident)
    super "movies", ident
  end

  def title
    get "title"
  end

  def title=(value)
    set "title", value
  end

  def director
    get "director"
  end
```

```
  def director=(value)
    set "director", value
  end
end
```

A Movie has two methods for each attribute: a reader, such as Movie#title, and a writer, such as Movie#title=. Bob can now load a new movie into the database by firing up the Ruby interactive interpreter and typing the following:

```
movie = Movie.new(1)
movie.title = "Doctor Strangelove"
movie.director = "Stanley Kubrick"
```

This code creates a new record in movies, which has values 1, Doctor Strangelove, and Stanley Kubrick for the columns id, title, and director, respectively. (Remember that in Ruby, movie.title = "Doctor Strangelove" is actually a disguised call to the method title=—the same as movie.title=("Doctor Strangelove").)

Proud of himself, Bob shows the code to his older, more experienced colleague, Bill. Bill stares at the screen for a few seconds and proceeds to shatter Bob's pride into tiny little pieces. "There's a lot of duplication in this code," Bill says. "You have a movies table with a title column in the database, and you have a Movie class with an @title field in the code. You also have a title method, a title= method, and two "title" string constants. You can solve this problem with way less code if you sprinkle some metaprogramming over it."

Enter Metaprogramming

At the suggestion of his expert-coder friend, Bob looks for a metaprogramming-based solution. He finds that very thing in the Active Record library, a popular Ruby library that maps objects to database tables. After a short tutorial, Bob is able to write the Active Record version of the Movie class:

```
class Movie < ActiveRecord::Base
end
```

Yes, it's as simple as that. Bob just subclassed the ActiveRecord::Base class. He didn't have to specify a table to map Movies to. Even better, he didn't have to write boring, almost identical methods such as title and director. It all just works:

```
movie = Movie.create
movie.title = "Doctor Strangelove"
movie.title  # => "Doctor Strangelove"
```

The previous code creates a Movie object that wraps a record in the movies table, then accesses the record's title column by calling Movie#title and Movie#title=.

But these methods are nowhere to be found in the source code. How can title and title= exist if they're not defined anywhere? You can find out by looking at how Active Record works.

The table name part is straightforward: Active Record looks at the name of the class through introspection and then applies some simple conventions. Since the class is named Movie, Active Record maps it to a table named movies. (This library knows how to find plurals for English words.)

What about methods such as title= and title, which access object attributes (*accessor methods* for short)? This is where metaprogramming comes in: Bob doesn't have to write those methods. Active Record defines them automatically, after inferring their names from the database schema. ActiveRecord::Base reads the schema at runtime, discovers that the movies table has two columns named title and director, and defines accessor methods for two attributes of the same name. This means that Active Record defines methods such as Movie#title and Movie#director= out of thin air while the program runs.

This is the "yang" to the introspection "yin": rather than just reading from the language constructs, you're writing into them. If you think this is an extremely powerful feature, you are right.

The "M" Word Again

Now you have a more formal definition of metaprogramming:

Metaprogramming is writing code that manipulates language constructs at runtime.

The authors of Active Record applied this concept. Instead of writing accessor methods for each class's attributes, they wrote code that defines those methods at runtime for *any* class that inherits from ActiveRecord::Base. This is what I meant when I talked about "writing code that writes code."

You might think that this is exotic, seldom-used stuff—but if you look at Ruby, as we're about to do, you'll see that it's used frequently.

Metaprogramming and Ruby

Remember our earlier talk about ghost towns and marketplaces? If you want to manipulate language constructs, those constructs must exist at runtime. In this respect, some languages are better than others. Take a quick glance at a few languages and how much control they give you at runtime.

A program written in C spans two different worlds: compile time, where you have language constructs such as variables and functions, and runtime,

Code Generators and Compilers

In metaprogramming, you write code that writes code. But isn't that what code generators and compilers do? For example, you can write annotated Java code and then use a code generator to output XML configuration files. In a broad sense, this XML generation is an example of metaprogramming. In fact, many people think about code generation when the "M" word comes up.

This particular brand of metaprogramming implies that you use a program to generate or otherwise manipulate a second, distinct program—and then you run the second program. After you run the code generator, you can actually read the generated code and (if you want to test your tolerance for pain) even modify it by hand before you finally run it. This is also what happens under the hood with C++ templates: the compiler turns your templates into a regular C++ program before compiling them, and then you run the compiled program.

In this book, I'll stick to a different meaning of *metaprogramming*, focusing on code that manipulates itself at runtime. You can think of this as *dynamic* metaprogramming to distinguish it from the *static* metaprogramming of code generators and compilers. While you can do some amount of dynamic metaprogramming in many languages (for example, by using bytecode manipulation in Java), only a few languages allow you do to it seamlessly and elegantly—and Ruby is one of them.

where you just have a bunch of machine code. Because most information from compile time is lost at runtime, C doesn't support metaprogramming or introspection. In C++, some language constructs do survive compilation, and that's why you can ask a C++ object for its class. In Java, the distinction between compile time and runtime is even fuzzier. You have enough introspection at your disposal to list the methods of a class or climb up a chain of superclasses.

Ruby is a very metaprogramming-friendly language. It has no compile time at all, and most constructs in a Ruby program are available at runtime. You don't come up against a brick wall dividing the code that you're writing from the code that your computer executes when you run the program. There is just one world.

In this one world, metaprogramming is everywhere. Ruby metaprogramming isn't an obscure art reserved for gurus, and it's not a bolt-on power feature that's useful only for building something as sophisticated as Active Record. If you want to take the path to advanced Ruby coding, you'll find metaprogramming at every step. Even if you're happy with the amount of Ruby you already know and use, you're still likely to stumble on metaprogramming in the source of popular frameworks, in your favorite library, and even in small examples from random blogs.

In fact, metaprogramming is so deeply entrenched in the Ruby language that it's not even sharply separated from "regular" programming. You can't look at a Ruby program and say, "This part here is metaprogramming, while this other part is not." In a sense, metaprogramming is a routine part of every Ruby programmer's job. Once you master it, you'll be able to tap into the full power of the language.

There is also another less obvious reason why you might want to learn metaprogramming. As simple as Ruby looks at first, you can quickly become overwhelmed by its subtleties. Sooner or later, you'll be asking yourself questions such as "Can an object call a private method on another object of the same class?" or "How can you define class methods by importing a module?" Ultimately, all of Ruby's seemingly complicated behaviors derive from a few simple rules. Through metaprogramming, you can get an intimate look at the language, learn those rules, and get answers to your nagging questions.

Now that you know what metaprogramming is about, you're ready to dive in.

## CHAPTER 2

Monday: The Object Model

Glance at any Ruby program, and you'll see objects everywhere. Do a double take, and you'll see that objects are citizens of a larger world that also includes other language constructs, such as classes, modules, and instance variables. Metaprogramming manipulates these language constructs, so you need to know a few things about them right off the bat.

You are about to dig into the first concept: all these constructs live together in a system called the *object model*. The object model is where you'll find answers to questions such as "Which class does this method come from?" and "What happens when I include this module?" Delving into the object model, at the very heart of Ruby, you'll learn some powerful techniques, and you'll also learn how to steer clear of a few pitfalls.

Monday promises to be a full day, so silence your messaging app, grab a donut, and get ready to start.

Open Classes

Where you refactor some legacy code and learn a trick or two along the way.

Welcome to your new job as a Ruby programmer. After you've settled yourself at your new desk with a shiny, latest-generation computer and a cup of coffee, you can meet Bill, your mentor. Yes, you have your first assignment at your new company, a new language to work with, and a new pair-programming buddy.

You've only been using Ruby for a few weeks, but Bill is there to help you. He has plenty of Ruby experience, and he looks like a nice guy. You're going to have a good time working with him—at least until your first petty fight over coding conventions.

The boss wants you and Bill to review the source of a small application called Bookworm. The company developed Bookworm to manage its large internal library of books. The program has slowly grown out of control as many different developers have added their pet features to the mix, from text previews to magazine management and the tracking of borrowed books. As a result, the Bookworm source code is a bit of a mess. You and Bill have been selected to go through the code and clean it up. The boss called it "just an easy refactoring job."

You and Bill have been browsing through the Bookworm source code for a few minutes when you spot your first refactoring opportunity. Bookworm has a function that formats book titles for printing on old-fashioned tape labels. It strips all punctuation and special characters out of a string, leaving only alphanumeric characters and spaces:

object_model/alphanumeric.rb

```
def to_alphanumeric(s)
  s.gsub(/[^\w\s]/, '')
end
```

This method also comes with its own unit test (remember to gem install test-unit before you try to run it on Ruby 2.2 and later):

```
require 'test/unit'

class ToAlphanumericTest < Test::Unit::TestCase
  def test_strip_non_alphanumeric_characters
    assert_equal '3 the Magic Number', to_alphanumeric('#3, the *Magic, Number*?')
  end
end
```

"This to_alphanumeric method is not very object oriented, is it?" Bill says. "This is generic functionality that makes sense for all strings. It'd be better if we could ask a String to convert itself, rather than pass it through an external method."

Even though you're the new guy on the block, you can't help but interrupt. "But this is just a regular String. To add methods to it, we'd have to write a whole new AlphanumericString class. I'm not sure it would be worth it."

"I think I have a simpler solution to this problem," Bill replies. He opens the String class and plants the to_alphanumeric method there:

```
class String
  def to_alphanumeric
    gsub(/[^\w\s]/, '')
  end
end
```

Bill also changes the callers to use String#to_alphanumeric. For example, the test becomes as follows:

```
require 'test/unit'

class StringExtensionsTest < Test::Unit::TestCase
  def test_strip_non_alphanumeric_characters
    assert_equal '3 the Magic Number', '#3, the *Magic, Number*?'.to_alphanumeric
  end
end
```

To understand the previous trick, you need to know a thing or two about Ruby classes. Bill is only too happy to teach you....

Inside Class Definitions

In Ruby, there is no real distinction between code that defines a class and code of any other kind. You can put any code you want in a class definition:

```
3.times do
  class C
    puts "Hello"
  end
end
```

```
‹ Hello
Hello
Hello
```

Ruby executed the code within the class just as it would execute any other code. Does that mean you defined three classes with the same name? The answer is no, as you can quickly find out yourself:

```
class D
  def x; 'x'; end
end

class D
  def y; 'y'; end
end

obj = D.new
obj.x          # => "x"
obj.y          # => "y"
```

When the previous code mentions class D for the first time, no class by that name exists yet. So, Ruby steps in and defines the class—and the x method. At the second mention, class D already exists, so Ruby doesn't need to define it. Instead, it reopens the existing class and defines a method named y there.

In a sense, the class keyword in Ruby is more like a scope operator than a class declaration. Yes, it creates classes that don't yet exist, but you might argue that it does this as a pleasant side effect. For class, the core job is to move you in the context of the class, where you can define methods.

This distinction about the class keyword is not an academic detail. It has an important practical consequence: you can always reopen existing classes— even standard library classes such as String or Array—and modify them on the fly. You can call this technique *Open Class*.

Spell: Open Class, page 239

To see how people use Open Classes in practice, let's look at a quick example from a real-life library.

The Monetize Example

You can find an example of Open Classes in the monetize gem, a library that deals with conversions of money and currencies. Here's how you create a Money object from a number:

```
object_model/monetize_example.rb
```

```ruby
require "monetize"

bargain_price = Monetize.from_numeric(99, "USD")
bargain_price.format # => "$99.00"
```

(The preceding code might not work out of the box for you, depending on the exact combination of Ruby and the monetize gem that you're using. However, the basic ideas stay the same for all versions.)

As a shortcut, you can also convert any number to a Money object by calling Numeric#to_money:

```ruby
require "monetize"

standard_price = 100.to_money("USD")
standard_price.format # => "$100.00"
```

Since Numeric is a standard Ruby class, you might wonder where the method Numeric#to_money comes from. Look through the source of the monetize gem, and you'll find code that reopens Numeric and defines that method:

```
gems/monetize-1.1.0/lib/monetize/core_extensions/numeric.rb
```

```ruby
class Numeric
  def to_money(currency = nil)
    Monetize.from_numeric(self, currency || Money.default_currency)
  end
end
```

It's quite common for libraries to use Open Classes this way.

As cool as they are, however, Open Classes have a dark side—one that you're about to experience.

The Problem with Open Classes

You and Bill don't have to look much further before you stumble upon another opportunity to use Open Classes. The Bookworm source contains a method that replaces elements in an array:

object_model/replace.rb

```
def replace(array, original, replacement)
  array.map {|e| e == original ? replacement : e }
end
```

Instead of focusing on the internal workings of replace, you can look at Bookworm's unit tests to see how that method is supposed to be used:

```
def test_replace
  original = ['one', 'two', 'one', 'three']
  replaced = replace(original, 'one', 'zero')
  assert_equal ['zero', 'two', 'zero', 'three'], replaced
end
```

This time, you know what to do. You grab the keyboard (taking advantage of Bill's slower reflexes) and move the method to the Array class:

```
class Array
  def replace(original, replacement)
    self.map {|e| e == original ? replacement : e }
  end
end
```

Then you change all calls to replace into calls to Array#replace. For example, the test becomes as follows:

```
def test_replace
  original = ['one', 'two', 'one', 'three']
➤ replaced = original.replace('one', 'zero')
  assert_equal ['zero', 'two', 'zero', 'three'], replaced
end
```

You save the test, you run Bookworm's unit tests suite, and...whoops! While test_replace does pass, other tests unexpectedly fail. To make things more perplexing, the failing tests seem to have nothing to do with the code you just edited. What gives?

"I think I know what happened," Bill says. He fires up irb, the interactive Ruby interpreter, and gets a list of all methods in Ruby's standard Array that begin with *re*:

```
[].methods.grep /^re/  # => [:reverse_each, :reverse, ..., :replace, ...]
```

In looking at the irb output, you spot the problem. Class Array already has a method named replace. When you defined your own replace method, you inadvertently overwrote the original replace, a method that some other part of Bookworm was relying on.

This is the dark side to Open Classes: if you casually add bits and pieces of functionality to classes, you can end up with bugs like the one you just encountered. Some people would frown upon this kind of reckless patching of classes, and they would refer to the previous code with a derogatory name: they'd call it a *Monkeypatch*.

Spell: Monkeypatch,
page 238

Now that you know what the problem is, you and Bill rename your own version of Array#replace to Array#substitute and fix both the tests and the calling code. You learned a lesson the hard way, but that didn't spoil your attitude. If anything, this incident piqued your curiosity about Ruby classes. It's time for you to learn the truth about them.

Inside the Object Model

Where you learn surprising facts about objects, classes, and constants.

Your recent experience with *Open Classes (14)* hints that there is more to Ruby classes than meets the eye. *Much* more, actually. Some of the truths about Ruby classes and the object model in general might even come as a bit of a shock when you first uncover them.

There is a lot to learn about the object model, but don't let all this theory put you off. If you understand the truth about classes and objects, you'll be well on your way to being a master of metaprogramming. Let's start with the basics: objects.

What's in an Object

Imagine running this code:

```ruby
class MyClass
  def my_method
    @v = 1
  end
end

obj = MyClass.new
obj.class            # => MyClass
```

Look at the obj object. If you could open the Ruby interpreter and look into obj, what would you see?

Is Monkeypatching Evil?

In the previous section, you learned that *Monkeypatch* is a derogatory term. However, the same term is sometimes used in a positive sense, to refer to *Open Classes (14)* in general. You might argue that there are two types of *Monkeypatches (16)*. Some happen by mistake, like the one that you and Bill experienced, and they're invariably evil. Others are applied on purpose, and they're quite useful—especially when you want to bend an existing library to your needs.

Even when you think you're in control, you should still Monkeypatch with care. Like any other global modification, Monkeypatches can be difficult to track in a large code base. To minimize the dangers of Monkeypatches, carefully check the existing methods in a class before you define your own methods. Also, be aware that some changes are riskier than others. For example, adding a new method is usually safer than modifying an existing one.

You'll see alternatives to Monkeypatching throughout the book. In particular, we will see soon that you can make Monkeypatches safer by using *Refinements (36)*. Unfortunately, Refinements are still a new feature, and there is no guarantee that they'll ever completely replace traditional Monkeypatches.

Instance Variables

Most importantly, objects contain instance variables. Even though you're not really supposed to peek at them, you can do that anyway by calling `Object#instance_variables`. The object from the previous example has just a single instance variable:

```
obj.my_method
obj.instance_variables  # => [:@v]
```

Unlike in Java or other static languages, in Ruby there is no connection between an object's class and its instance variables. Instance variables just spring into existence when you assign them a value, so you can have objects of the same class that carry different instance variables. For example, if you hadn't called `obj.my_method`, then `obj` would have no instance variable at all. You can think of the names and values of instance variables as keys and values in a hash. Both the keys and the values can be different for each object.

That's all there is to know about instance variables. Let's move on to methods.

Methods

Besides having instance variables, objects also have methods. You can get a list of an object's methods by calling `Object#methods`. Most objects (including `obj` in the previous example) inherit a number of methods from `Object`, so this list of methods is usually quite long. You can use Array#grep to check that my_method is in obj's list:

```
obj.methods.grep(/my/)   # => [:my_method]
```

If you could pry open the Ruby interpreter and look into obj, you'd notice that this object doesn't really carry a list of methods. An object contains its instance variables and a reference to a class (because every object belongs to a class, or—in OO speak—is an *instance* of a class)...but no methods. Where are the methods?

Your pair-programming buddy Bill walks over to the nearest whiteboard and starts scribbling all over it. "Think about it for a minute," he says, drawing the following diagram. "Objects that share the same class also share the same methods, so the methods must be stored in the class, not the object."

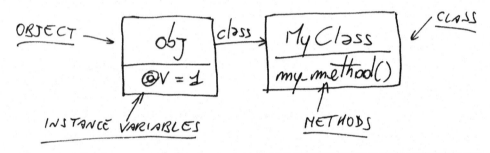

Figure 1—Instance variables live in objects; methods live in classes.

Before going on, you should be aware of one important distinction about methods. You can rightly say that "obj has a method called my_method," meaning that you're able to call obj.my_method(). By contrast, you shouldn't say that "MyClass has a method named my_method." That would be confusing, because it would imply that you're able to call MyClass.my_method() as if it were a class method.

To remove the ambiguity, you should say that my_method is an *instance method* (not just "a method") of MyClass, meaning that it's defined in MyClass, and you actually need an object (or *instance*) of MyClass to call it. It's the same method, but when you talk about the class, you call it an *instance method*, and when you talk about the object, you simply call it a *method*. Remember this distinction, and you won't get confused when writing introspective code like this:

```
String.instance_methods == "abc".methods   # => true
String.methods == "abc".methods            # => false
```

Let's wrap it all up: an object's instance variables live in the object itself, and an object's methods live in the object's class. That's why objects of the same class share methods but don't share instance variables.

That's all you really have to know about objects, instance variables, and methods. But since we brought classes into the picture, we can also take a closer look at them.

The Truth About Classes

Here is possibly the most important thing you'll ever learn about the Ruby object model: *classes themselves are nothing but objects.*

Because a class is an object, everything that applies to objects also applies to classes. Classes, like any object, have their own class, called—you guessed it—Class:

```
"hello".class    # => String
String.class     # => Class
```

You might be familiar with Class from other object-oriented languages. In languages such as Java, however, an instance of Class is just a read-only description of the class. By contrast, a Class in Ruby is quite literally the class itself, and you can manipulate it like you would manipulate any other object. For example, in Chapter 5, *Thursday: Class Definitions*, on page 105, you'll see that you can call Class.new to create new classes while your program is running. This flexibility is typical of Ruby's metaprogramming: while other languages allow you to read class-related information, Ruby allows you to *write* that information at runtime.

Like any object, classes also have methods. Remember what you learned in *What's in an Object*, on page 16? The methods of an object are also the instance methods of its class. In turn, this means that the methods of a class are the instance methods of Class:

```
# The "false" argument here means: ignore inherited methods
Class.instance_methods(false)    # => [:allocate, :new, :superclass]
```

You already know about new because you use it all the time to create objects. The allocate method plays a supporting role to new. Chances are, you'll never need to care about it.

On the other hand, you'll use the superclass method a lot. This method is related to a concept that you're probably familiar with: inheritance. A Ruby class *inherits* from its superclass. Have a look at the following code:

```
Array.superclass        # => Object
Object.superclass       # => BasicObject
BasicObject.superclass  # => nil
```

The Array class inherits from Object, which is the same as saying "an array is an object." Object contains methods that are generally useful for any object— such as to_s, which converts an object to a string. In turn, Object inherits from BasicObject, the root of the Ruby class hierarchy, which contains only a few essential methods. (You will learn more about BasicObject later in the book.)

While talking about superclasses, we can ask ourselves one more question: what is the superclass of Class?

Modules

Take a deep breath and check out the superclass of the Class class itself:

```
Class.superclass        # => Module
```

The superclass of Class is Module—which is to say, every class is also a module. To be precise, a class is a module with three additional instance methods (new, allocate, and superclass) that allow you to create objects or arrange classes into hierarchies.

Indeed, classes and modules are so closely related that Ruby could easily get away with a single "thing" that plays both roles. The main reason for having a distinction between modules and classes is clarity: by carefully picking either a class or a module, you can make your code more explicit. Usually, you pick a module when you mean it to be included somewhere, and you pick a class when you mean it to be instantiated or inherited. So, although you can use classes and modules interchangeably in many situations, you'll probably want to make your intentions clear by using them for different purposes.

Putting It All Together

Bill concludes his lecture with a piece of code and a whiteboard diagram:

```
class MyClass; end
obj1 = MyClass.new
obj2 = MyClass.new
```

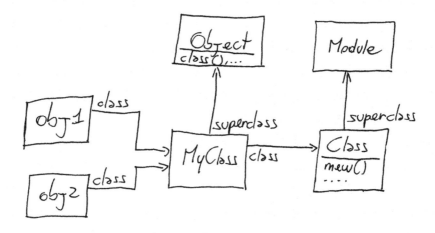

Figure 2—Classes are just objects.

"See?" Bill asks, pointing at the previous diagram. "Classes and regular objects live together happily."

There's one more interesting detail in the "Classes are objects" theme: like you do with any other object, you hold onto a class with a *reference*. A variable can reference a class just like any other object:

```
my_class = MyClass
```

MyClass and my_class are both references to the same instance of Class—the only difference being that my_class is a variable, while MyClass is a constant. To put this differently, just as classes are nothing but objects, class names are nothing but constants. So let's look more closely at constants.

Constants

Any reference that begins with an uppercase letter, including the names of classes and modules, is a *constant*. You might be surprised to learn that a Ruby constant is actually very similar to a variable—to the extent that you can change the value of a constant, although you will get a warning from the interpreter. (If you're in a destructive mood, you can even break Ruby beyond repair by changing the value of the String class name.)

If you can change the value of a constant, how is a constant different from a variable? The one important difference has to do with their scope. The scope of constants follows its own special rules, as you can see in the example that follows.

```ruby
module MyModule
  MyConstant = 'Outer constant'

  class MyClass
    MyConstant = 'Inner constant'
  end
end
```

Bill pulls a napkin from his shirt pocket and sketches out the constants in this code. You can see the result in the following figure.

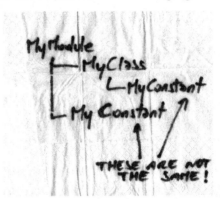

All the constants in a program are arranged in a tree similar to a file system, where modules (and classes) are *directories* and regular constants are *files*. Like in a file system, you can have multiple files with the same name, as long as they live in different directories. You can even refer to a constant by its *path*, as you'd do with a file. Let's see how.

The Paths of Constants

You just learned that constants are nested like directories and files. Also like directories and files, constants are uniquely identified by their paths. Constants' paths use a double colon as a separator (this is akin to the scope operator in C++):

```ruby
module M
  class C
    X = 'a constant'
  end
  C::X # => "a constant"
end

M::C::X # => "a constant"
```

If you're sitting deep inside the tree of constants, you can provide the absolute path to an outer constant by using a leading double colon as root:

```ruby
Y = 'a root-level constant'
```

```
module M
  Y = 'a constant in M'
  Y        # => "a constant in M"
  ::Y      # => "a root-level constant"
end
```

The Module class also provides an instance method and a class method that, confusingly, are both called constants. Module#constants returns all constants in the current scope, like your file system's ls command (or dir command, if you're running Windows). Module.constants returns all the top-level constants in the current program, including class names:

```
M.constants                      # => [:C, :Y]
Module.constants.include? :Object  # => true
Module.constants.include? :Module  # => true
```

Finally, if you need the current path, check out Module.nesting:

```
module M
  class C
    module M2
      Module.nesting     # => [M::C::M2, M::C, M]
    end
  end
end
```

The similarities between Ruby constants and files go even further: you can use modules to organize your constants, the same way that you use directories to organize your files. Let's look at an example.

The Rake Example

The earliest versions of Rake, the popular Ruby build system, defined classes with obvious names, such as Task and FileTask. These names had a good chance of clashing with other class names from different libraries. To prevent clashes, Rake switched to defining those classes inside a Rake module:

gems/rake-0.9.2.2/lib/rake/task.rb

```
module Rake
  class Task
    # ...
```

Now the full name of the Task class is Rake::Task, which is unlikely to clash with someone else's name. A module such as Rake, which only exists to be a container of constants, is called a *Namespace*.

Spell: Namespace, page 238

This switch to Namespaces had a problem: if someone had an old Rake build file lying around—one that still referenced the earlier, non-Namespaced class names—that file wouldn't work with an upgraded version of Rake. For this reason, Rake maintained compatibility with older build files for a while. It did so by providing a command-line option named classic-namespace that loaded an additional source file. This source file assigned the new, safer constant names to the old, unsafe ones:

gems/rake-0.9.2.2/lib/rake/classic_namespace.rb

```
Task = Rake::Task
FileTask = Rake::FileTask
FileCreationTask = Rake::FileCreationTask
# ...
```

When this file was loaded, both Task and Rake::Task ended up referencing the same instance of Class, so a build file could use either constant to refer to the class. A few versions afterwards, Rake assumed that all users had migrated their build file, and it removed the option.

Enough digression on constants. Let's go back to objects and classes, and wrap up what you've just learned.

Objects and Classes Wrap-Up

What's an object? It's a bunch of instance variables, plus a link to a class. The object's methods don't live in the object—they live in the object's class, where they're called the *instance methods* of the class.

What's a class? It's an object (an instance of Class), plus a list of instance methods and a link to a superclass. Class is a subclass of Module, so a class is also a module. If this is confusing, look back at Figure 2, *Classes are just objects*, on page 21.

These are instance methods of the Class class. Like any object, a class has its own methods, such as new. Also like any object, classes must be accessed through references. You already have a constant reference to each class: the class's name.

"That's pretty much all there is to know about objects and classes," Bill says. "If you can understand this, you're well on your way to understanding metaprogramming. Now, let's turn back to the code."

Using Namespaces

It takes only a short while for you to get a chance to apply your newfound knowledge about classes. Sifting through the Bookworm source code, you stumble upon a class that represents a snippet of text out of a book:

```
class TEXT
  # ...
```

Ruby class names are conventionally Pascal cased: words are concatenated with the first letter of each capitalized: ThisTextIsPascalCased, so you rename the class Text:

```
class Text
```

You change the name of the class everywhere it's used, you run the unit tests, and—surprise!—the tests fail with a cryptic error message:

```
TypeError: Text is not a class
```

"D'oh! Of course it is," you exclaim. Bill is as puzzled as you are, so it takes the two of you some time to find the cause of the problem. As it turns out, the Bookworm application requires an old version of the popular Action Mailer library. Action Mailer, in turn, uses a text-formatting library that defines a module named—you guessed it—Text:

```
module Text
```

That's where the problem lies: because Text is already the name of a module, Ruby complains that it can't also be the name of a class at the same time.

In a sense, you were lucky that this name clash was readily apparent. If Action Mailer's Text had been a class, you might have never noticed that this name already existed. Instead, you'd have inadvertently *Monkeypatched (16)* the existing Text class. At that point, only your unit tests would have protected you from potential bugs.

Fixing the clash between your Text class and Action Mailer's Text module is as easy as wrapping your class in a *Namespace (23)*:

```
module Bookworm
  class Text
```

You and Bill also change all references to Text into references to Bookworm::Text. It's unlikely that an external library defines a class named Bookworm::Text, so you should be safe from clashes now.

That was a lot of learning in a single sitting. You deserve a break and a cup of coffee—and a little quiz.

Quiz: Missing Lines

Where you find your way around the Ruby object model.

Back in *The Truth About Classes*, on page 19, Bill showed you how objects and classes are related. As an example, he used a snippet of code and this whiteboard diagram:

Loading and Requiring

Speaking of *Namespaces (23)*, there is one interesting detail that involves Namespaces, constants, and Ruby's load and require methods. Imagine finding a motd.rb file on the web that displays a "message of the day" on the console. You want to add this code to your latest program, so you load the file to execute it and display the message:

```
load('motd.rb')
```

Using load, however, has a side effect. The motd.rb file probably defines variables and classes. Although variables fall out of scope when the file has finished loading, constants don't. As a result, motd.rb can pollute your program with the names of its own constants—in particular, class names.

You can force motd.rb to keep its constants to itself by passing a second, optional argument to load:

```
load('motd.rb', true)
```

If you load a file this way, Ruby creates an anonymous module, uses that module as a Namespace to contain all the constants from motd.rb, and then destroys the module.

The require method is quite similar to load, but it's meant for a different purpose. You use load to execute code, and you use require to import libraries. That's why require has no second argument: those leftover class names are probably the reason why you imported the file in the first place. Also, that's why require tries only once to load each file, while load executes the file again every time you call it.

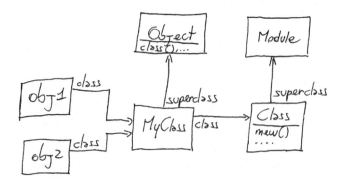

```
class MyClass; end
obj1 = MyClass.new
obj2 = MyClass.new
```

The diagram shows some of the connections between the program entities. Now it's your turn to add more lines and boxes to the diagram and answer these questions:

- What's the class of Object?
- What's the superclass of Module?
- What's the class of Class?
- Imagine that you execute this code:

```
obj3 = MyClass.new
obj3.instance_variable_set("@x", 10)
```

Can you add obj3 to the diagram?

You can use irb and the Ruby documentation to find out the answers.

Quiz Solution

Your enhanced version of the original diagram is in Figure 3, *Bill's diagram, enhanced by you*, on page 28.

As you can easily check in irb, the superclass of Module is Object. You don't even need irb to know what the class of Object is: because Object is a class, its class must be Class. This is true of all classes, meaning that the class of Class must be Class itself. Don't you love self-referential logic?

Finally, calling instance_variable_set blesses obj3 with its own instance variable @x. If you find this concept surprising, remember that in a dynamic language such as Ruby, every object has its own list of instance variables, independent of other objects—even other objects of the same class.

What Happens When You Call a Method?

Where you learn that a humble method call requires a lot of work on Ruby's part and you shed light on a twisted piece of code.

After some hours working on Bookworm, you and Bill already feel confident enough to fix some minor bugs here and there—but now, as your working day is drawing to a close, you find yourself stuck. Attempting to fix a long-standing bug, you've stumbled upon a tangle of classes, modules, and methods that you can't make heads or tails of.

"Stop!" Bill shouts, startling you. "This code is too complicated. To understand it, you have to learn in detail what happens when you call a method." And before you can react, he dives into yet another lecture.

When you call a method, Ruby does two things:

1. It finds the method. This is a process called *method lookup*.

2. It executes the method. To do that, Ruby needs something called self.

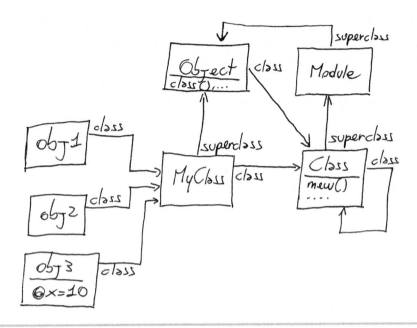

Figure 3—Bill's diagram, enhanced by you

This process—find a method and then execute it—happens in every object-oriented language. In Ruby, however, you should understand the process in depth, because this knowledge will open the door to some powerful tricks. We'll talk about method lookup first, and we'll come around to self later.

Method Lookup

You already know about the simplest case of method lookup. Look back at Figure 1, *Instance variables live in objects; methods live in classes*, on page 18. When you call a method, Ruby looks into the object's class and finds the method there. Before you look at a more complicated example, though, you need to know about two new concepts: the receiver and the ancestors chain.

The *receiver* is the object that you call a method on. For example, if you write my_string.reverse(), then my_string is the receiver.

To understand the concept of an *ancestors chain*, look at any Ruby class. Then imagine moving from the class into its superclass, then into the superclass's superclass, and so on, until you reach BasicObject, the root of the Ruby class hierarchy. The path of classes you just traversed is the ancestors chain of the class. (The ancestors chain also includes modules, but forget about them for now. We'll get around to modules in a bit.)

Now that you know what a receiver is and what an ancestors chain is, you can sum up the process of method lookup in a single sentence: to find a method, Ruby goes in the receiver's class, and from there it climbs the ancestors chain until it finds the method. Here's an example:

`object_model/lookup.rb`

```ruby
class MyClass
  def my_method; 'my_method()'; end
end

class MySubclass < MyClass
end

obj = MySubclass.new
obj.my_method()          # => "my_method()"
```

Bill draws this diagram:

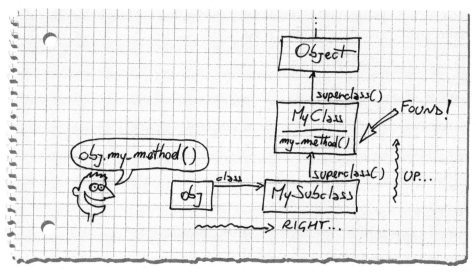

If you're used to traditional class diagrams, this picture might look confusing to you. Why is obj, a humble object, hanging around in the same diagram with a class hierarchy? Don't get confused—this is not a class diagram. Every box in the diagram is an object. It's just that some of these objects happen to be classes, and classes are linked together through the superclass method.

When you call my_method, Ruby goes *right* from obj, the receiver, into MySubclass. Because it can't find my_method there, Ruby continues its search by going *up* into MyClass, where it finally finds the method.

MyClass doesn't specify a superclass, so it implicitly inherits from the default superclass: Object. If it hadn't found the method in MyClass, Ruby would look for the method by climbing up the chain into Object and finally BasicObject.

Because of the way most people draw diagrams, this behavior is also called the "one step to the right, then up" rule: go *one step to the right* into the receiver's class, and then go *up* the ancestors chain until you find the method. You can ask a class for its ancestors chain with the ancestors method:

```
MySubclass.ancestors # => [MySubclass, MyClass, Object, Kernel, BasicObject]
```

"Hey, what's Kernel doing there in the ancestors chain?" you ask. "You told me about a chain of superclasses, but I'm pretty sure that Kernel is a module, not a class."

"You're right." Bill admits. "I forgot to tell you about modules. They're easy...."

Modules and Lookup

You learned that the ancestors chain goes from class to superclass. Actually, the ancestors chain also includes modules. When you include a module in a class (or even in another module), Ruby inserts the module in the ancestors chain, right above the including class itself:

object_model/modules_include.rb

```ruby
module M1
  def my_method
    'M1#my_method()'
  end
end

class C
  include M1
end

class D < C; end

D.ancestors # => [D, C, M1, Object, Kernel, BasicObject]
```

Starting from Ruby 2.0, you also have a second way to insert a module in a class's chain of ancestors: the prepend method. It works like include, but it inserts the module *below* the including class (sometimes called the *includer*), rather than above it:

```ruby
class C2
  prepend M2
end

class D2 < C2; end

D2.ancestors # => [D2, M2, C2, Object, Kernel, BasicObject]
```

Bill draws the following flowchart to show how include and prepend work.

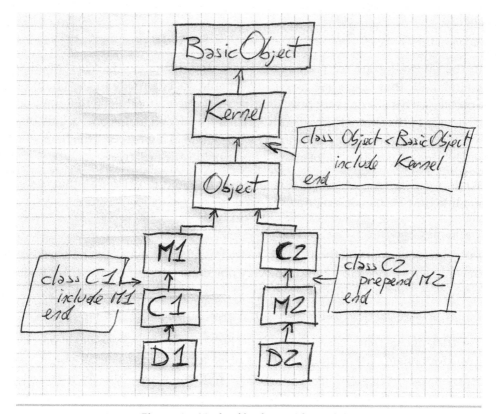

Figure 4—Method lookup with modules

Later in this book, you'll see how to use prepend to your advantage. For now, it's enough that you understand the previous diagram. There is one last corner case about include and prepend, however—one that is worth mentioning right away.

Multiple Inclusions

What happens if you try to include a module in the same chain of ancestors multiple times? Here is an example:

object_model/modules_multiple.rb

```ruby
module M1; end

module M2
  include M1
end

module M3
  prepend M1
  include M2
```

end

```
M3.ancestors # => [M1, M3, M2]
```

In the previous code, M3 prepends M1 and then includes M2. When M2 also includes M1, that include has no effect, because M1 is already in the chain of ancestors. This is true every time you include or prepend a module: if that module is already in the chain, Ruby silently ignores the second inclusion. As a result, a module can appear only once in the same chain of ancestors. This behavior might change in future Rubies—but don't hold your breath.

While we're talking about modules, it's worth taking a look at that Kernel module that keeps popping up everywhere.

The Kernel

Ruby includes some methods, such as print, that you can call from anywhere in your code. It looks like each and every object has the print method. Methods such as print are actually private instance methods of module Kernel:

```
Kernel.private_instance_methods.grep(/^pr/) # => [:printf, :print, :proc]
```

The trick here is that class Object includes Kernel, so Kernel gets into every object's ancestors chain. Every line of Ruby is always executed inside an object, so you can call the instance methods in Kernel from anywhere. This gives you the illusion that print is a language keyword, when it's actually a method. Neat, isn't it?

Spell: Kernel Method, page 237

You can take advantage of this mechanism yourself: if you add a method to Kernel, this *Kernel Method* will be available to all objects. To prove that Kernel Methods are actually useful, you can look at the way some Ruby libraries use them.

The Awesome Print Example

The awesome_print gem prints Ruby objects on the screen with indentation, color, and other niceties:

`object_model/awesome_print_example.rb`

```
require "awesome_print"
local_time = {:city => "Rome", :now => Time.now }
ap local_time, :indent => 2
```

This produces:

```
{
    :city => "Rome",
    :now => 2013-11-30 12:51:03 +0100
```

```
}
```

You can call ap from anywhere because it's a *Kernel Method (32)*, which you can verify by peeking into Awesome Print's source code:

gems/awesome_print-1.1.0/lib/awesome_print/core_ext/kernel.rb

```
module Kernel
  def ap(object, options = {})
    # ...
  end
end
```

After this foray into Ruby modules and the Kernel, you can finally learn how Ruby executes methods after finding them.

Method Execution

When you call a method, Ruby does two things: first, it finds the method, and second, it executes the method. Up to now, you focused on the finding part. Now you can finally look at the execution part.

Imagine being the Ruby interpreter. Somebody called a method named, say, my_method. You found the method by going one step to the right, then up, and it looks like this:

```
def my_method
  temp = @x + 1
  my_other_method(temp)
end
```

To execute this method, you need to answer two questions. First, what object does the instance variable @x belong to? And second, what object should you call my_other_method on?

Being a smart human being (as opposed to a dumb computer program), you can probably answer both questions intuitively: both @x and my_other_method belong to the *receiver*—the object that my_method was originally called upon. However, Ruby doesn't have the luxury of intuition. When you call a method, it needs to tuck away a reference to the receiver. Thanks to this reference, it can remember who the receiver is as it executes the method.

That reference to the receiver can be useful for you as well—so it is worth exploring further.

The self Keyword

Every line of Ruby code is executed inside an object—the so-called *current object*. The current object is also known as self, because you can access it with the self keyword.

Only one object can take the role of self at a given time, but no object holds that role for a long time. In particular, when you call a method, the receiver becomes self. From that moment on, all instance variables are instance variables of self, and all methods called without an explicit receiver are called on self. As soon as your code explicitly calls a method on some other object, that other object becomes self.

Here is an artfully complicated example to show you self in action:

object_model/self.rb

```ruby
class MyClass
  def testing_self
    @var = 10        # An instance variable of self
    my_method()      # Same as self.my_method()
    self
  end

  def my_method
    @var = @var + 1
  end
end

obj = MyClass.new
obj.testing_self  # => #<MyClass:0x007f93ab08a728 @var=11>
```

As soon as you call testing_self, the receiver obj becomes self. Because of that, the instance variable @var is an instance variable of obj, and the method my_method is called on obj. As my_method is executed, obj is still self, so @var is still an instance variable of obj. Finally, testing_self returns a reference to self. (You can also check the output to verify that @var is now 11.)

If you want to become a master of Ruby, you should always know which object has the role self at any given moment. In most cases, that's easy: just track which object was the last method receiver. However, there are two important special cases that you should be aware of. Let's look at them.

The Top Level

You just learned that every time you call a method on an object, that object becomes self. But then, who's self if you haven't called any method yet? You can run irb and ask Ruby itself for an answer:

```ruby
self        # => main
```

What private Really Means

Now that you know about self, you can cast a new light on Ruby's private keyword. Private methods are governed by a single simple rule: you cannot call a private method with an explicit receiver. In other words, every time you call a private method, it must be on the implicit receiver—self. Let's see a corner case:

```ruby
class C
  def public_method
    self.private_method
  end

  private

  def private_method; end
end

C.new.public_method
```

```
❮ NoMethodError: private method 'private_method' called [...]
```

You can make this code work by removing the self keyword.

This contrived example shows that private methods come from two rules working together: first, you need an explicit receiver to call a method on an object that is not yourself, and second, private methods can be called only with an implicit receiver. Put these two rules together, and you'll see that you can only call a private method on yourself. You can call this the "private rule."

You could find Ruby's private methods perplexing—especially if you come from Java or C#, where private behaves differently. When you're in doubt, go back to the private rule, and everything will make sense. Can object x call a private method on object y if the two objects share the same class? The answer is no, because no matter which class you belong to, you still need an explicit receiver to call another object's method. Can you call a private method that you inherited from a superclass? The answer is yes, because you don't need an explicit receiver to call inherited methods on yourself.

```ruby
self.class  # => Object
```

As soon as you start a Ruby program, you're sitting within an object named main that the Ruby interpreter created for you. This object is sometimes called the *top-level context*, because it's the object you're in when you're at the top level of the call stack: either you haven't called any method yet or all the methods that you called have returned. (Oh, and in case you're wondering, Ruby's main has nothing to do with the main() functions in C and Java.)

Class Definitions and self

In a class or module definition (and outside of any method), the role of self is taken by the class or module itself.

```ruby
class MyClass
```

```
self          # => MyClass
end
```

This last detail is not going to be useful right now, but it will become a central concept later in this book. For now, we can set it aside and go back to the main topic.

Everything that you've learned so far about method execution can be summed up in a few short sentences. When you call a method, Ruby looks up the method by following the "one step to the right, then up" rule and then executes the method with the receiver as self. There are some special cases in this procedure (for example, when you include a module), but there are no exceptions…except for one.

Refinements

Remember the first refactoring you coded today, in *Open Classes*, on page 11? You and Bill used an *Open Class (14)* to add a method to Strings:

object_model/alphanumeric.rb

```
class String
  def to_alphanumeric
    gsub(/[^\w\s]/, '')
  end
end
```

The problem with modifying classes this way is that the changes are global: from the moment the previous code is executed, every String in the system gets the changes. If the change is an incompatible *Monkeypatch (16)*, you might break some unrelated code—as happened to you and Bill when you inadvertently redefined Array#replace.

Spell: Refinement, page 240 Starting with Ruby 2.0, you can deal with this problem using a *Refinement*. Begin by writing a module and calling refine inside the module definition:

object_model/refinements_in_file.rb

```
module StringExtensions
  refine String do
    def to_alphanumeric
      gsub(/[^\w\s]/, '')
    end
  end
end
```

This code refines the String class with a new to_alphanumeric method. Differently from a regular Open Class, however, a Refinement is not active by default. If you try to call String#to_alphanumeric, you'll get an error:

```
"my *1st* refinement!".to_alphanumeric
```

‹ NoMethodError: undefined method `to_alphanumeric' [...]

To activate the changes, you have to do so explicitly, with the using method:

```
using StringExtensions
```

From the moment you call using, all the code in that Ruby source file will see the changes:

```
"my *1st* refinement!".to_alphanumeric   # => "my 1st refinement"
```

Starting from Ruby 2.1, you can even call using inside a module definition. The Refinement will be active until the end of the module definition. The code below patches the String#reverse method—but only for the code inside the definition of StringStuff:

object_model/refinements_in_module.rb
```
module StringExtensions
  refine String do
    def reverse
      "esrever"
    end
  end
end

module StringStuff
  using StringExtensions
  "my_string".reverse    # => "esrever"
end

"my_string".reverse      # => "gnirts_ym"
```

Refinements are similar to Monkeypatches, but they're not global. A Refinement is active in only two places: the refine block itself and the code starting from the place where you call using until the end of the module (if you're in a module definition) or the end of the file (if you're at the top level)

In the limited scope where it's active, a Refinement is just as good as an Open Class or a Monkeypatch. It can define new methods, redefine existing methods, include or prepend modules, and generally do anything that a regular Open Class can do. Code in an active Refinement takes precedence over code in the refined class, and also over code in modules that are included or prepended by the class. Refining a class is like slapping a patch right onto the original code of the class.

On the other hand, because they're not global, Refinements don't have the issues that you experienced in *The Problem with Open Classes*, on page 15.

You can apply a Refinement to a few selected areas of your code, and the rest of your code will stick with the original unrefined class—so there aren't many chances that you'll break your system by inadvertently impacting unrelated code. However, this local quality of Refinements has the potential to surprise you, as you're about to find out.

Refinement Gotchas

Look at this code:

object_model/refinements_gotcha.rb

```ruby
class MyClass
  def my_method
    "original my_method()"
  end

  def another_method
    my_method
  end
end

module MyClassRefinement
  refine MyClass do
    def my_method
      "refined my_method()"
    end
  end
end

using MyClassRefinement
MyClass.new.my_method       # => "refined my_method()"
MyClass.new.another_method  # => "original my_method()"
```

The call to my_method happens after the call to using, so you get the refined version of the method, just like you expect. However, the call to another_method could catch you off guard: even if you call another_method after using, the call to my_method itself happens *before* using—so it calls the original, unrefined version of the method.

Some people find the result above counterintuitive. The lesson here is to double-check your method calls when you use *Refinements (36)*. Also keep in mind that Refinements are still an evolving feature—so much so that Ruby 2.0 issues a scary warning when your program uses Refinements for the first time:

```
warning: Refinements are experimental, and the
behavior may change in future versions of Ruby!
```

This warning has been removed in Ruby 2.1, but there are still a few corner cases where Refinements might not behave as you expect—and some of those corner cases might change in future Rubies. For example, you can call refine in a regular module, but you cannot call it in a class, even if a class is itself a module. Also, metaprogramming methods such as methods and ancestors ignore Refinements altogether. Behaviors such as these have sound technical justifications, but they could trip you up nonetheless. Refinements have the potential to eliminate dangerous Monkeypatches, but it will take some time for the Ruby community to understand how to use them best.

You're still considering the power and responsibility of using Refinements when Bill decides to throw a quiz at you.

Quiz: Tangle of Modules

Where you untangle a twisted yarn of modules, classes, and objects.

You can finally go back to the problem that prompted Bill to launch into his discussion on method lookup, self, and Refinements. You've had trouble making sense of a complicated arrangement of classes and modules. Here's the confusing part:

object_model/tangle.rb

```ruby
module Printable
  def print
    # ...
  end

  def prepare_cover
    # ...
  end
end

module Document
  def print_to_screen
    prepare_cover
    format_for_screen
    print
  end

  def format_for_screen
    # ...
  end

  def print
    # ...
  end
end
```

```
class Book
  include Document
  include Printable
  # ...
end
```

Another source file creates a Book and calls print_to_screen:

```
b = Book.new
b.print_to_screen
```

According to the company's bug management application, there is a problem with this code: print_to_screen is not calling the right print method. The bug report doesn't provide anymore details.

Can you guess which version of print gets called—the one in Printable or the one in Document? Try drawing the chain of ancestors on paper. How can you quickly fix the code so print_to_screen calls the other version of print instead?

Quiz Solution

You can ask Ruby itself for the ancestors chain of Book:

```
Book.ancestors  # => [Book, Printable, Document, Object, Kernel, BasicObject]
```

If you draw this ancestors chain on your whiteboard, it will look like Figure 5, *The ancestors chain of the Book class*, on page 41.

Let's see how Ruby builds the chain. Because Book doesn't have an explicit superclass, it implicitly inherits from Object, which in turn includes Kernel and inherits from BasicObject. When Book includes Document, Ruby adds Document to Book's ancestors chain right above Book itself. Immediately after that, Book includes Printable. Again, Ruby slips Printable in the chain right above Book, pushing up the rest of the chain—from Document upward.

When you call b.print_to_screen, the object referenced by b becomes self, and method lookup begins. Ruby finds the print_to_screen method in Document, and that method then calls other methods—including print. All methods called without an explicit receiver are called on self, so method lookup starts once again from Book (self's class) and goes up until it finds a method named print. The lowest print in the chain is Printable#print, so that's the one that gets called.

The bug report hints that the original author of the code intended to call Document#print instead. In real production code, you'd probably want to get rid of this confusion and rename one of the clashing print methods. However, if you just want to solve this quiz, the cheapest way to do it is to swap the order

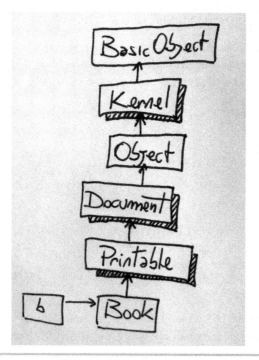

Figure 5—The ancestors chain of the Book class

of inclusion of the modules in Book so that Document gets lower than Printable in the ancestors chain:

object_model/tangle_untwisted.rb

```ruby
module Printable
  # ...
end

module Document
  # ...
end

class Book
  include Printable
  include Document

  ancestors  # => [Book, Document, Printable, Object, Kernel, BasicObject]
end
```

The implicit receiver of ancestors in the previous code is Book, because in a class definition the role of self is taken by the class. The ancestors chain of Book also contains a third method named print—but Bill is not telling you where it is. If you're curious, you'll have to find it yourself, maybe with some help from your friend irb.

It's almost time to go home after an exhausting but very satisfying day of work. But before you call it a day, Bill does a complete wrap-up of what you learned.

Wrap-Up

Here's a checklist of what you learned today:

- An object is composed of a bunch of instance variables and a link to a class.

- The methods of an object live in the object's class. (From the point of view of the class, they're called *instance methods*.)

- The class itself is just an object of class Class. The name of the class is just a constant.

- Class is a subclass of Module. A module is basically a package of methods. In addition to that, a class can also be instantiated (with new) or arranged in a hierarchy (through its superclass).

- Constants are arranged in a tree similar to a file system, where the names of modules and classes play the part of directories and regular constants play the part of files.

- Each class has an ancestors chain, beginning with the class itself and going up to BasicObject.

- When you call a method, Ruby goes *right* into the class of the receiver and then *up* the ancestors chain, until it either finds the method or reaches the end of the chain.

- When you include a module in a class, the module is inserted in the ancestors chain right *above* the class itself. When you prepend the module, it is inserted in the ancestors chain right *below* the class.

- When you call a method, the receiver takes the role of self.

- When you're defining a module (or a class), the module takes the role of self.

- Instance variables are always assumed to be instance variables of self.

- Any method called without an explicit receiver is assumed to be a method of self.

- Refinements are like pieces of code patched right over a class, and they override normal method lookup. On the other hand, a Refinement works in a limited area of the program: the lines of code between the call to using and the end of the file, or the end of the module definition.

Checked...checked...done! Now it's time to go home before your brain explodes with all the information you crammed into it today.

## CHAPTER 3

Tuesday: Methods

Yesterday you learned about the Ruby object model and how to make Ruby classes sing and dance for you. Today you're holding all calls to focus on *methods*.

The objects in your code talk to each other all the time. Some languages—such as Java and C—feature a compiler that presides over this chatting. For every method call, the compiler checks to see that the receiving object has a matching method. This is called *static type checking*, and the languages that adopt it are called *static languages*. For example, if you call talk_simple on a Lawyer object that has no such method, the compiler protests loudly.

Dynamic languages—such as Python and Ruby—don't have a compiler policing method calls. As a consequence, you can start a program that calls talk_simple on a Lawyer, and everything works just fine—that is, until that specific line of code is executed. Only then does the Lawyer complain that it doesn't understand that call.

That's an important advantage of static type checking: the compiler can spot some of your mistakes before the code runs. This protectiveness, however, comes at a price. Static languages often require you to write lots of tedious, repetitive methods—the so-called *boilerplate methods*—just to make the compiler happy. (For example, get and set methods to access an object's properties, or scores of methods that do nothing but delegate to some other object.)

In Ruby, boilerplate methods aren't a problem, because you can easily avoid them with techniques that would be impractical or just plain impossible in a static language. In this chapter, we'll focus on those techniques.

A Duplication Problem

Where you and Bill face a problem with duplicated code.

Today, your boss asked you to work on a program for the purchasing department. They want a system that flags expenses greater than $99 for computer gear, so they can crack down on developers splurging with company money. (You read that right: *$99*. The purchasing department isn't fooling around.)

Some other developers already took a stab at the project, coding a report that lists all the components of each computer in the company and how much each component costs. To date, they haven't plugged in any real data. Here's where you and Bill come in.

The Legacy System

Right from the start, you have a challenge on your hands: the data you need to load into the already established program is stored in a legacy system stuck behind an awkwardly coded class named DS (for "data source"):

methods/computer/data_source.rb

```
class DS
  def initialize # connect to data source...
  def get_cpu_info(workstation_id) # ...
  def get_cpu_price(workstation_id) # ...
  def get_mouse_info(workstation_id) # ...
  def get_mouse_price(workstation_id) # ...
  def get_keyboard_info(workstation_id) # ...
  def get_keyboard_price(workstation_id) # ...
  def get_display_info(workstation_id) # ...
  def get_display_price(workstation_id) # ...
  # ...and so on
```

DS#initialize connects to the data system when you create a new DS object. The other methods—and there are dozens of them—take a workstation identifier and return descriptions and prices for the computer's components. With Bill standing by to offer moral support, you quickly try the class in irb:

```
ds = DS.new
ds.get_cpu_info(42)     # => "2.9 Ghz quad-core"
ds.get_cpu_price(42)    # => 120
ds.get_mouse_info(42)   # => "Wireless Touch"
ds.get_mouse_price(42)  # => 60
```

It looks like workstation number 42 has a 2.9GHz CPU and a luxurious $60 mouse. This is enough data to get you started.

Double, Treble... Trouble

You have to wrap DS into an object that fits the reporting application. This means each Computer must be an object. This object has a single method for each component, returning a string that describes both the component and its price. Remember that price limit set by the purchasing department? Keeping this requirement in mind, you know that if the component costs $100 or more, the string must begin with an asterisk to draw people's attention.

You kick off development by writing the first three methods in the Computer class:

methods/computer/duplicated.rb

```ruby
class Computer
  def initialize(computer_id, data_source)
    @id = computer_id
    @data_source = data_source
  end

  def mouse
    info = @data_source.get_mouse_info(@id)
    price = @data_source.get_mouse_price(@id)
    result = "Mouse: #{info} ($#{price})"
    return "* #{result}" if price >= 100
    result
  end

  def cpu
    info = @data_source.get_cpu_info(@id)
    price = @data_source.get_cpu_price(@id)
    result = "Cpu: #{info} ($#{price})"
    return "* #{result}" if price >= 100
    result
  end

  def keyboard
    info = @data_source.get_keyboard_info(@id)
    price = @data_source.get_keyboard_price(@id)
    result = "Keyboard: #{info} ($#{price})"
    return "* #{result}" if price >= 100
    result
  end

  # ...
end
```

At this point in the development of Computer, you find yourself bogged down in a swampland of repetitive copy and paste. You have a long list of methods left to deal with, and you should also write tests for each and every method, because it's easy to make mistakes in duplicated code.

"I can think of two different ways to remove this duplication," Bill says. "One is a spell called Dynamic Methods. The other is a special method called method_missing. We can try both solutions and decide which one we like better." You agree to start with Dynamic Methods and get to method_missing after that.

Dynamic Methods

Where you learn how to call and define methods dynamically, and you remove the duplicated code.

"When I was a young developer learning C++," Bill says, "my mentors told me that when you call a method, you're actually sending a message to an object. It took me a while to get used to that concept. If I'd been using Ruby back then, that notion of sending messages would have come more naturally to me."

Calling Methods Dynamically

When you call a method, you usually do so using the standard dot notation:

methods/dynamic_call.rb

```ruby
class MyClass
  def my_method(my_arg)
    my_arg * 2
  end
end

obj = MyClass.new
obj.my_method(3)   # => 6
```

You also have an alternative: call MyClass#my_method using Object#send in place of the dot notation:

```ruby
obj.send(:my_method, 3)    # => 6
```

The previous code still calls my_method, but it does so through send. The first argument to send is the message that you're sending to the object—that is, a symbol or a string representing the name of a method. (See *Method Names and Symbols,* on page 49.) Any remaining arguments (and the block, if one exists) are simply passed on to the method.

Why would you use send instead of the plain old dot notation? Because with send, the name of the method that you want to call becomes just a regular argument. You can wait literally until the very last moment to decide which method to call, *while* the code is running. This technique is called *Dynamic Dispatch,* and you'll find it wildly useful. To help reveal its magic, let's look at a couple of real-life examples.

Spell: Dynamic Dispatch, page 234

Method Names and Symbols

People who are new to the language are sometimes confused by Ruby's symbols. Symbols and strings belong to two separate and unrelated classes:

```
:x.class  # => Symbol
"x".class # => String
```

Nevertheless, symbols are similar enough to strings that you might wonder what's the point of having symbols at all. Can't you just use regular strings everywhere?

There are a few different reasons to use symbols in place of regular strings, but in the end the choice boils down to conventions. In most cases, symbols are used as names of things—in particular, names of metaprogramming-related things such as methods. Symbols are a good fit for such names because they are *immutable*: you can change the characters inside a string, but you can't do that for symbols. You wouldn't expect the name of a method to change, so it makes sense to use a symbol when you refer to a method name.

For example, when you call Object#send, you need to pass it the name of a method as a first argument. Although send accepts this name as either a symbol or a string, symbols are usually considered more kosher:

```
# rather than: 1.send("+", 2)
1.send(:+, 2)   # => 3
```

Regardless, you can easily convert from string to symbol and back:

```
"abc".to_sym   #=> :abc
:abc.to_s      #=> "abc"
```

The Pry Example

One example of Dynamic Dispatch comes from Pry. Pry is a popular alternative to irb, Ruby's command-line interpreter. A Pry object stores the interpreter's configuration into its own attributes, such as memory_size and quiet:

methods/pry_example.rb

```
require "pry"

pry = Pry.new
pry.memory_size = 101
pry.memory_size        # => 101
pry.quiet = true
```

For each instance method like Pry#memory_size, there is a corresponding class method (Pry.memory_size) that returns the default value of the attribute:

```
Pry.memory_size        # => 100
```

Let's look a little deeper inside the Pry source code. To configure a Pry instance, you can call a method named Pry#refresh. This method takes a hash that maps attribute names to their new values:

```
pry.refresh(:memory_size => 99, :quiet => false)
pry.memory_size          # => 99
pry.quiet                # => false
```

Pry#refresh has a lot of work to do: it needs to go through each attribute (such as self.memory_size); initialize the attribute with its default value (such as Pry.memory_size); and finally check whether the hash argument contains a new value for the same attribute, and if it does, set the new value. Pry#refresh could do all of those steps with code like this:

```
def refresh(options={})
  defaults[:memory_size] = Pry.memory_size
  self.memory_size = options[:memory_size] if options[:memory_size]

  defaults[:quiet] = Pry.quiet
  self.quiet = options[:quiet] if options[:quiet]
  # same for all the other attributes...
end
```

Those two lines of code would have to be repeated for each and every attribute. That's a lot of duplicated code. Pry#refresh manages to avoid that duplication, and instead uses *Dynamic Dispatch (48)* to set all the attributes with just a few lines of code:

gems/pry-0.9.12.2/lib/pry/pry_instance.rb

```
def refresh(options={})
  defaults    = {}
  attributes = [ :input, :output, :commands, :print, :quiet,
                 :exception_handler, :hooks, :custom_completions,
                 :prompt, :memory_size, :extra_sticky_locals ]

  attributes.each do |attribute|
    defaults[attribute] = Pry.send attribute
  end
  # ...
  defaults.merge!(options).each do |key, value|
    send("#{key}=", value) if respond_to?("#{key}=")
  end

  true
end
```

The code above uses send to read the default attribute values into a hash, merges this hash with the options hash, and finally uses send again to call attribute accessors such as memory_size=. The Kernel#respond_to? method returns true if methods such as Pry#memory_size= actually exist, so that any key in options that doesn't match an existing attribute will be ignored. Neat, huh?

Privacy Matters

Remember what Spiderman's uncle used to say? "With great power comes great responsibility." The Object#send method is very powerful—perhaps *too* powerful. In particular, you can call any method with send, including private methods.

If that kind of breaching of encapsulation makes you uneasy, you can use public_send instead. It's like send, but it makes a point of respecting the receiver's privacy. Be prepared, however, for the fact that Ruby code in the wild rarely bothers with this concern. If anything, a lot of Ruby programmers use send exactly *because* it allows calling private methods, not in spite of that.

Now you know about send and Dynamic Dispatch—but there is more to Dynamic Methods than that. You're not limited to calling methods dynamically. You can also *define* methods dynamically. It's time to see how.

Defining Methods Dynamically

You can define a method on the spot with Module#define_method. You just need to provide a method name and a block, which becomes the method body:

methods/dynamic_definition.rb

```ruby
class MyClass
  define_method :my_method do |my_arg|
    my_arg * 3
  end
end

obj = MyClass.new
obj.my_method(2)   # => 6
```

define_method is executed within MyClass, so my_method is defined as an instance method of MyClass. This technique of defining a method at runtime is called a *Dynamic Method.*

Spell: Dynamic Method, page 235

There is one important reason to use define_method over the more familiar def keyword: define_method allows you to decide the name of the defined method at runtime. To see an example of this technique, look back at your original refactoring problem.

Refactoring the Computer Class

Recall the code that pulled you and Bill into this dynamic discussion:

methods/computer/duplicated.rb

```ruby
class Computer
  def initialize(computer_id, data_source)
    @id = computer_id
    @data_source = data_source
  end

  def mouse
    info = @data_source.get_mouse_info(@id)
    price = @data_source.get_mouse_price(@id)
    result = "Mouse: #{info} ($#{price})"
    return "* #{result}" if price >= 100
    result
  end

  def cpu
    info = @data_source.get_cpu_info(@id)
    price = @data_source.get_cpu_price(@id)
    result = "Cpu: #{info} ($#{price})"
    return "* #{result}" if price >= 100
    result
  end

  def keyboard
    info = @data_source.get_keyboard_info(@id)
    price = @data_source.get_keyboard_price(@id)
    result = "Keyboard: #{info} ($#{price})"
    return "* #{result}" if price >= 100
    result
  end

  # ...
end
```

In the previous pages you learned how to use Module#define_method in place of the def keyword to define a method, and how to use send in place of the dot notation to call a method. Now you can use these spells to refactor the Computer class. It's time to remove some duplication.

Step 1: Adding Dynamic Dispatches

You and Bill start by extracting the duplicated code into its own message-sending method:

methods/computer/dynamic_dispatch.rb

```ruby
class Computer
  def initialize(computer_id, data_source)
    @id = computer_id
    @data_source = data_source
  end

  def mouse
```

```
➤      component :mouse
➤    end
➤
➤    def cpu
➤      component :cpu
➤    end
➤
➤    def keyboard
➤      component :keyboard
➤    end
➤
➤    def component(name)
➤      info = @data_source.send "get_#{name}_info", @id
➤      price = @data_source.send "get_#{name}_price", @id
➤      result = "#{name.capitalize}: #{info} ($#{price})"
➤      return "* #{result}" if price >= 100
➤      result
➤    end
    end
```

A call to mouse is delegated to component, which in turn calls DS#get_mouse_info and DS#get_mouse_price. The call also writes the capitalized name of the component in the resulting string. You open an irb session and smoke-test the new Computer:

```
my_computer = Computer.new(42, DS.new)
my_computer.cpu   # => * Cpu: 2.16 Ghz ($220)
```

This new version of Computer is a step forward because it contains far fewer duplicated lines—but you still have to write dozens of similar methods. To avoid writing all those methods, you can turn to define_method.

Step 2: Generating Methods Dynamically

You and Bill refactor Computer to use *Dynamic Methods (51)*, as shown in the following code.

methods/computer/dynamic_methods.rb

```
class Computer
  def initialize(computer_id, data_source)
    @id = computer_id
    @data_source = data_source
  end

  def self.define_component(name)
    define_method(name) do
      info = @data_source.send "get_#{name}_info", @id
      price = @data_source.send "get_#{name}_price", @id
      result = "#{name.capitalize}: #{info} ($#{price})"
      return "* #{result}" if price >= 100
      result
    end
  end

  define_component :mouse
  define_component :cpu
  define_component :keyboard
end
```

Note that the three calls to define_component are executed inside the definition of Computer, where Computer is the implicit self. Because you're calling define_component on Computer, you have to make it a class method.

You quickly test the slimmed-down Computer class in irb and discover that it still works. It's time to move on to the next step.

Step 3: Sprinkling the Code with Introspection

The latest Computer contains minimal duplication, but you can push it even further and remove the duplication altogether. How? By getting rid of all those calls to define_component. You can do that by introspecting the data_source argument and extracting the names of all components:

methods/computer/more_dynamic_methods.rb

```
class Computer
  def initialize(computer_id, data_source)
    @id = computer_id
    @data_source = data_source
    data_source.methods.grep(/^get_(.*)_info$/) { Computer.define_component $1 }
  end

  def self.define_component(name)
    define_method(name) do
      # ...
    end
  end
end
```

The new line in initialize is where the magic happens. To understand it, you need to know a couple of things.

First, if you pass a block to Array#grep, the block is evaluated for each element that matches the regular expression. Second, the string matching the parenthesized part of the regular expression is stored in the global variable $1. So, if data_source has methods named get_cpu_info and get_mouse_info, this code ultimately calls Computer.define_component twice, with the strings "cpu" and "mouse". Note that define_method works equally well with a string or a symbol.

The duplicated code is finally gone for good. As a bonus, you don't even have to write or maintain the list of components. If someone adds a new component to DS, the Computer class will support it automatically. Isn't that wonderful?

Let's Try That Again

Your refactoring was a resounding success, but Bill is not willing to stop here. "We said that we were going to try *two* different solutions to this problem, remember? We've only found one, involving *Dynamic Dispatch (48)* and *Dynamic Methods (51)*. It did serve us well—but to be fair, we need to give the other solution a chance."

For this second solution, you need to know about some strange methods that are not really methods and a very special method named method_missing.

method_missing

Where you listen to spooky stories about Ghost Methods and dynamic proxies and you try a second way to remove duplicated code.

With Ruby, there's no compiler to enforce method calls. This means you can call a method that doesn't exist. For example:

methods/method_missing.rb

```
class Lawyer; end
nick = Lawyer.new
nick.talk_simple
```

‹ NoMethodError: undefined method `talk_simple' for #<Lawyer:0x007f801aa81938>

Do you remember how method lookup works? When you call talk_simple, Ruby goes into nick's class and browses its instance methods. If it can't find talk_simple there, it searches up the ancestors chain into Object and eventually into BasicObject.

Because Ruby can't find talk_simple anywhere, it admits defeat by calling a method named method_missing on nick, the original receiver. Ruby knows that method_missing is there, because it's a private instance method of BasicObject that every object inherits.

You can experiment by calling method_missing yourself. It's a private method, but you can get to it through send:

```
nick.send :method_missing, :my_method
```

❮ NoMethodError: undefined method `my_method' for #<Lawyer:0x007f801b0f4978>

You have just done exactly what Ruby does. You told the object, "I tried to call a method named my_method on you, and you did not understand." BasicObject#method_missing responded by raising a NoMethodError. In fact, this is what method_missing does for a living. It's like an object's dead-letter office, the place where unknown messages eventually end up (and the place where NoMethodErrors come from).

Overriding method_missing

Most likely, you will never need to call method_missing yourself. Instead, you can override it to intercept unknown messages. Each message landing on method_missing's desk includes the name of the method that was called, plus any arguments and blocks associated with the call.

methods/more_method_missing.rb

```ruby
class Lawyer
  def method_missing(method, *args)
    puts "You called: #{method}(#{args.join(', ')})"
    puts "(You also passed it a block)" if block_given?
  end
end

bob = Lawyer.new
bob.talk_simple('a', 'b') do
  # a block
end
```

❮ You called: talk_simple(a, b)
  (You also passed it a block)

Overriding method_missing allows you to call methods that don't really exist. Let's take a closer look at these weird creatures.

Ghost Methods

When you need to define many similar methods, you can spare yourself the definitions and just respond to calls through method_missing. This is like saying to the object, "If they ask you something and you don't understand, do this."

From the caller's side, a message that's processed by method_missing looks like a regular call—but on the receiver's side, it has no corresponding method. This trick is called a *Ghost Method*. Let's look at some Ghost Method examples.

Spell: Ghost Method, page 236

The Hashie Example

The Hashie gem contains a little bit of magic called Hashie::Mash. A Mash is a more powerful version of Ruby's standard OpenStruct class: a hash-like object whose attributes work like Ruby variables. If you want a new attribute, just assign a value to the attribute, and it will spring into existence:

```
require 'hashie'

icecream = Hashie::Mash.new
icecream.flavor = "strawberry"
icecream.flavor                # => "strawberry"
```

This works because Hashie::Mash is a subclass of Ruby's Hash, and its attributes are actually Ghost Methods, as a quick look at Hashie::Mash.method_missing will confirm:

gems/hashie-1.2.0/lib/hashie/mash.rb

```
module Hashie
  class Mash < Hashie::Hash
    def method_missing(method_name, *args, &blk)
      return self.[](method_name, &blk) if key?(method_name)
      match = method_name.to_s.match(/(.*?)([?=!]?)$/)
      case match[2]
      when "="
        self[match[1]] = args.first
        # ...
      else
        default(method_name, *args, &blk)
      end
    end

    # ...
  end
end
```

If the name of the called method is the name of a key in the hash (such as flavor), then Hashie::Mash#method_missing simply calls the [] method to return the corresponding value. If the name ends with a "=", then method_missing chops off the "=" at the end to get the attribute name and then stores its value. If the name of the called method doesn't match any of these cases, then method_missing just returns a default value. (Hashie::Mash also supports a few other special cases, such as methods ending in "?", that were scrapped from the code above.)

Dynamic Proxies

Ghost Methods (57) are usually icing on the cake, but some objects actually rely almost exclusively on them. These objects are often wrappers for something else—maybe another object, a web service, or code written in a different language. They collect method calls through method_missing and forward them to the wrapped object. Let's look at a complex real-life example.

The Ghee Example

You probably know GitHub,[1] the wildly popular social coding service. A number of libraries give you easy access to GitHub's HTTP APIs, including a Ruby gem called Ghee. Here is how you use Ghee to access a user's "gist"— a snippet of code that can be published on GitHub:

methods/ghee_example.rb

```ruby
require "ghee"

gh = Ghee.basic_auth("usr", "pwd")  # Your GitHub username and password
all_gists = gh.users("nusco").gists
a_gist = all_gists[20]

a_gist.url              # => "https://api.github.com/gists/535077"
a_gist.description      # => "Spell: Dynamic Proxy"

a_gist.star
```

The code above connects to GitHub, looks up a specific user ("nusco"), and accesses that user's list of gists. Then it selects one specific gist and reads that gist's url and description. Finally, it "stars" the gist, to be notified of any future changes.

The GitHub APIs expose tens of types of objects besides gists, and Ghee has to support all of those objects. However, Ghee's source code is surprisingly concise, thanks to a smart use of *Ghost Methods (57)*. Most of the magic happens in the Ghee::ResourceProxy class:

gems/ghee-0.9.8/lib/ghee/resource_proxy.rb

```ruby
class Ghee
  class ResourceProxy
    # ...

    def method_missing(message, *args, &block)
      subject.send(message, *args, &block)
    end

    def subject
      @subject ||= connection.get(path_prefix){|req| req.params.merge!params }.body
```

---

1. http://www.github.com

```
    end
  end
end
```

Before you understand this class, you need to see how Ghee uses it. For each type of GitHub object, such as *gists* or *users*, Ghee defines one subclass of Ghee::ResourceProxy. Here is the class for gists (the class for users is quite similar):

gems/ghee-0.9.8/lib/ghee/api/gists.rb

```ruby
class Ghee
  module API
    module Gists
      class Proxy < ::Ghee::ResourceProxy
        def star
          connection.put("#{path_prefix}/star").status == 204
        end

        # ...

    end
  end
end
```

When you call a method that changes the state of an object, such as Ghee::API::Gists#star, Ghee places an HTTP call to the corresponding GitHub URL. However, when you call a method that just reads from an attribute, such as url or description, that call ends into Ghee::ResourceProxy#method_missing. In turn, method_missing forwards the call to the object returned by Ghee::ResourceProxy#subject. What kind of object is that?

If you dig into the implementation of ResourceProxy#subject, you'll find that this method also makes an HTTP call to the GitHub API. The specific call depends on which subclass of Ghee::ResourceProxy we're using. For example, Ghee::API::Gists::Proxy calls https://api.github.com/users/nusco/gists. ResourceProxy#subject receives the GitHub object in JSON format—in our example, all the gists of user *nusco*—and converts it to a hash-like object.

Dig a little deeper, and you'll find that this hash-like object is actually a Hashie::Mash, the magic hash class that we talked about in *The Hashie Example*, on page 57. This means that a method call such as my_gist.url is forwarded to Ghee::ResourceProxy#method_missing, and from there to Hashie::Mash#method_missing, which finally returns the value of the url attribute. Yes, that's two calls to method_missing in a row.

Ghee's design is elegant, but it uses so much metaprogramming that it might confuse you at first. Let's wrap it up in just two points:

- Ghee stores GitHub objects as dynamic hashes. You can access the attributes of these hashes by calling their *Ghost Methods (57)*, such as url and description.

- Ghee also wraps these hashes inside proxy objects that enrich them with additional methods. A proxy does two things. First, it implements methods that require specific code, such as star. Second, it forwards methods that just read data, such as url, to the wrapped hash.

Thanks to this two-level design, Ghee manages to keep its code very compact. It doesn't need to define methods that just read data, because those methods are Ghost Methods. Instead, it can just define the methods that need specific code, like star.

This dynamic approach also has another advantage: Ghee can adapt automatically to some changes in the GitHub APIs. For example, if GitHub added a new field to gists (say, lines_count), Ghee would support calls to Ghee::API::Gists#lines_count without any changes to its source code, because lines_count is just a Ghost Method—actually a chain of *two* Ghost Methods.

An object such as Ghee::ResourceProxy, which catches Ghost Methods and forwards them to another object, is called a *Dynamic Proxy.*

Spell: Dynamic Proxy, page 235

Refactoring the Computer Class (Again)

"Okay, you now know about method_missing," Bill says. "Let's go back to the Computer class and remove the duplication."

Once again, here's the original Computer class:

methods/computer/duplicated.rb

```
class Computer
  def initialize(computer_id, data_source)
    @id = computer_id
    @data_source = data_source
  end

  def mouse
    info = @data_source.get_mouse_info(@id)
    price = @data_source.get_mouse_price(@id)
    result = "Mouse: #{info} ($#{price})"
    return "* #{result}" if price >= 100
    result
  end

  def cpu
    info = @data_source.get_cpu_info(@id)
    price = @data_source.get_cpu_price(@id)
    result = "Cpu: #{info} ($#{price})"
```

```
      return "* #{result}" if price >= 100
      result
    end

    def keyboard
      info = @data_source.get_keyboard_info(@id)
      price = @data_source.get_keyboard_price(@id)
      result = "Keyboard: #{info} ($#{price})"
      return "* #{result}" if price >= 100
      result
    end

    # ...
end
```

Computer is just a wrapper that collects calls, tweaks them a bit, and routes them to a data source. To remove all those duplicated methods, you can turn Computer into a Dynamic Proxy. It only takes an override of method_missing to remove all the duplication from the Computer class.

`methods/computer/method_missing.rb`

```
class Computer
    def initialize(computer_id, data_source)
      @id = computer_id
      @data_source = data_source
    end

➤   def method_missing(name)
➤     super if !@data_source.respond_to?("get_#{name}_info")
➤     info = @data_source.send("get_#{name}_info", @id)
➤     price = @data_source.send("get_#{name}_price", @id)
➤     result = "#{name.capitalize}: #{info} ($#{price})"
➤     return "* #{result}" if price >= 100
➤     result
➤   end
end
```

What happens when you call a method such as Computer#mouse? The call gets routed to method_missing, which checks whether the wrapped data source has a get_mouse_info method. If it doesn't have one, the call falls back to BasicObject#method_missing, which throws a NoMethodError. If the data source knows about the component, the original call is converted into two calls to DS#get_mouse_info and DS#get_mouse_price. The values returned from these calls are used to build the final result. You try the new class in irb:

```
my_computer = Computer.new(42, DS.new)
my_computer.cpu   # => * Cpu: 2.9 Ghz quad-core ($120)
```

It worked. Bill, however, is concerned about one last detail.

respond_to_missing?

If you specifically ask a Computer whether it responds to a Ghost Method, it will flat-out lie:

```
cmp = Computer.new(0, DS.new)
cmp.respond_to?(:mouse)          # => false
```

This behavior can be problematic, because respond_to? is a commonly used method. (If you need convincing, just note that the Computer itself is calling respond_to? on the data source.) Fortunately, Ruby provides a clean mechanism to make respond_to? aware of Ghost Methods.

respond_to? calls a method named respond_to_missing? that is supposed to return true if a method is a Ghost Method. (In your mind, you could rename respond_to_missing? to something like ghost_method?.) To prevent respond_to? from lying, override respond_to_missing? every time you override method_missing:

```
class Computer
  # ...

➤  def respond_to_missing?(method, include_private = false)
➤    @data_source.respond_to?("get_#{method}_info") || super
➤  end
end
```

The code in this respond_to_missing? is similar to the first line of method_missing: it finds out whether a method is a Ghost Method. If it is, it returns true. If it isn't, it calls super. In this case, super is the default Object#respond_to_missing?, which always returns false.

Now respond_to? will learn about your Ghost Methods from respond_to_missing? and return the right result:

```
cmp.respond_to?(:mouse)    # => true
```

Back in the day, Ruby coders used to override respond_to? directly. Now that respond_to_missing? is available, overriding respond_to? is considered somewhat dirty. Instead, the rule is now this: remember to override respond_to_missing? every time you override method_missing.

If you like BasicObject#method_missing, you should also take a look at Module#const_missing. Let's check it out.

const_missing

Remember our discussion of Rake in *The Rake Example*, on page 23? In that section we said that at one point in its history, Rake renamed classes like Task to names that are less likely to clash, such as Rake::Task. After renaming the classes, Rake went through an upgrade path: for a few versions, you could use either the new class names or the old, non-Namespaced names. Rake allowed you to do that by *Monkepatching (16)* the Module#const_missing method:

gems/rake-0.9.2.2/lib/rake/ext/module.rb

```ruby
class Module
  def const_missing(const_name)
    case const_name
    when :Task
      Rake.application.const_warning(const_name)
      Rake::Task
    when :FileTask
      Rake.application.const_warning(const_name)
      Rake::FileTask
    when :FileCreationTask
      # ...
    end
  end
end
```

When you reference a constant that doesn't exist, Ruby passes the name of the constant to const_missing as a symbol. Class names are just constants, so a reference to an unknown Rake class such as Task was routed to Module#const_missing. In turn, const_missing warned you that you were using an obsolete class name:

methods/const_missing.rb

```ruby
require 'rake'
task_class = Task
```

```
WARNING: Deprecated reference to top-level constant 'Task' found [...]
    Use --classic-namespace on rake command
    or 'require "rake/classic_namespace"' in Rakefile
```

After the warning, you automatically got the new, Namespaced class name in place of the old one:

```ruby
task_class        # => Rake::Task
```

Enough talking about magic methods. Let's recap what you and Bill did today.

Refactoring Wrap-Up

Today you solved the same problem in two different ways. The first version of Computer introspects DS to get a list of methods to wrap and uses *Dynamic Methods (51)* and *Dynamic Dispatches (48)*, which delegate to the legacy system. The second version of Computer does the same with *Ghost Methods (57)*. Having to pick one of the two versions, you and Bill randomly select the method_missing-based one, send it to the folks in purchasing, and head out for a well-deserved lunch break...and an unexpected quiz.

Quiz: Bug Hunt

Where you discover that bugs in a method_missing can be difficult to squash.

Over lunch, Bill has a quiz for you. "My previous team followed a cruel office ritual," he says. "Every morning, each team member picked a random number. Whoever got the smallest number had to take a trip to the nearby Starbucks and buy coffee for the whole team."

Bill explains that the team even wrote a class that was supposed to provide a random number (and some *Wheel of Fortune*–style suspense) when you called the name of a team member. Here's the class:

methods/roulette_failure.rb

```ruby
class Roulette
  def method_missing(name, *args)
    person = name.to_s.capitalize
    3.times do
      number = rand(10) + 1
      puts "#{number}..."
    end
    "#{person} got a #{number}"
  end
end
```

You can use the Roulette like this:

```ruby
number_of = Roulette.new
puts number_of.bob
puts number_of.frank
```

And here's what the result is supposed to look like:

```
5...
6...
10...
Bob got a 3
7...
4...
3...
Frank got a 10
```

"This code was clearly overdesigned," Bill admits. "We could have just defined a regular method that took the person's name as a string—but we'd just discovered method_missing, so we used *Ghost Methods (57)* instead. That wasn't a good idea; the code didn't work as expected."

Can you spot the problem with the Roulette class? If you can't, try running it on your computer. Now can you explain what is happening?

Quiz Solution

The Roulette contains a bug that causes an infinite loop. It prints a long list of numbers and finally crashes.

```
2...
7...
1...
5...
(...more numbers here...)
roulette_failure.rb:7:in `method_missing': stack level too deep (SystemStackError)
```

This bug is nasty and difficult to spot. The variable number is defined within a block (the block that gets passed to times) and falls out of scope by the last line of method_missing. When Ruby executes that line, it can't know that the number there is supposed to be a variable. As a default, it assumes that number must be a parentheses-less method call on self.

In normal circumstances, you would get an explicit NoMethodError that makes the problem obvious. But in this case you have a method_missing, and that's where the call to number ends. The same chain of events happens again—and again and again—until the call stack overflows.

This is a common problem with Ghost Methods: because unknown calls become calls to method_missing, your object might accept a call that's just plain wrong. Finding a bug like this one in a large program can be pretty painful.

To avoid this kind of trouble, take care not to introduce too many Ghost Methods. For example, Roulette might be better off if it simply accepted the names of people on Frank's team. Also, remember to fall back on BasicObject#method_missing when you get a call you don't know how to handle. Here's a better Roulette that still uses method_missing:

methods/roulette_solution.rb

```ruby
class Roulette
  def method_missing(name, *args)
    person = name.to_s.capitalize
    super unless %w[Bob Frank Bill].include? person
    number = 0
    3.times do
      number = rand(10) + 1
      puts "#{number}..."
    end
    "#{person} got a #{number}"
```

```
    end
end
```

You can also develop this code in bite-sized steps. Start by writing regular methods; then, when you're confident that your code is working, refactor the methods to a method_missing. This way, you won't inadvertently hide a bug behind a Ghost Method.

Blank Slates

Where you and Bill learn to avoid another common method_missing trap.

Once you get back from lunch, you find an unexpected problem waiting for you at the office. The developer who wrote the reporting application stumbled upon what he thinks is "the strangest bug ever": the Computer class can't retrieve information about the workstations' displays. All the other methods work fine, but Computer#display doesn't.

You try the display method in irb, and sure enough it fails:

```
my_computer = Computer.new(42, DS.new)
my_computer.display      # => nil
```

Why does Computer#display return nil? You triple-check the code and the back-end data source, but everything seems to be fine. Bill has a sudden insight, and he lists the instance methods of Object that begin with a *d*:

```
Object.instance_methods.grep /^d/    # => [:dup, :display, :define_singleton_method]
```

It seems that Object defines a method named display (a seldom-used method that prints an object on a port and always returns nil). Computer inherits from Object, so it gets the display method. The call to Computer#display finds a real method by that name, so it never lands on method_missing. You're calling a real, live method instead of a *Ghost Method (57)*.

This problem crops up with *Dynamic Proxies (60)*. When the name of a Ghost Method clashes with the name of a real, inherited method, the latter wins.

If you don't need the inherited method, you can fix the problem by removing it. While you're at it, you might want to remove most methods from the class, preventing such name clashes from ever happening again. A skinny class with a minimal number of methods is called a *Blank Slate*. As it turns out, Ruby has a ready-made Blank Slate for you to use.

Spell: Blank Slate, page 232

BasicObject

The root of Ruby's class hierarchy, BasicObject, has only a handful of instance methods:

methods/basic_object.rb

```
im = BasicObject.instance_methods
im # => [:==, :equal?, :!, :!=, :instance_eval, :instance_exec, :__send__, :__id__]
```

If you don't specify a superclass, your classes inherit by default from Object, which is itself a subclass of BasicObject. If you want a *Blank Slate (66)*, you can inherit directly from BasicObject instead. For example, if Computer inherited directly from BasicObject, then it wouldn't have a problematic display method.

Inheriting from BasicObject is the quicker way to define a Blank Slate in Ruby. In some cases, however, you might want to control exactly which methods to keep and which methods to remove from your class. Let's see how you can remove a specific method from a class.

Removing Methods

You can remove a method from a class by using either Module#undef_method or Module#remove_method. The drastic undef_method removes any method, including the inherited ones. The kinder remove_method removes the method from the receiver, but it leaves inherited methods alone. Let's look at a real-life library that uses undef_method to create a Blank Slate.

The Builder Example

The Builder gem is an XML generator with a twist. You can generate XML tags by calling methods on Builder::XmlMarkup:

methods/builder_example_1.rb

```
require 'builder'
xml = Builder::XmlMarkup.new(:target=>STDOUT, :indent=>2)

xml.coder {
  xml.name 'Matsumoto', :nickname => 'Matz'
  xml.language 'Ruby'
}
```

This code produces the following snippet of XML:

```
<coder>
  <name nickname="Matz">Matsumoto</name>
  <language>Ruby</language>
</coder>
```

Builder cleverly bends the syntax of Ruby to support nested tags, attributes, and other niceties. The core idea of Builder is simple: calls such as name and language are processed by XmlMarkup#method_missing, which generates an XML tag for every call.

Now pretend you have to generate a piece of XML describing a university course. It might look like this:

```
<semester>
  <class>Egyptology</class>
  <class>Ornithology</class>
</semester>
```

So, you'd have to write code like this:

methods/builder_example_2.rb

```
xml.semester {
  xml.class 'Egyptology'
  xml.class 'Ornithology'
}
```

If XmlMarkup were a subclass of Object, then the calls to class would clash with Object's class. To avoid that clash, XmlMarkup inherits from a *Blank Slate (66)* that removes class and most other methods from Object. When Builder was written, BasicObject didn't exist yet. (It was introduced in Ruby 1.9.) So Builder defines its own Blank Slate class:

gems/builder-3.2.2/lib/blankslate.rb

```
class BlankSlate
  # Hide the method named +name+ in the BlankSlate class.  Don't
  # hide +instance_eval+ or any method beginning with "__".
  def self.hide(name)
    # ...
    if instance_methods.include?(name._blankslate_as_name) &&
        name !~ /^(__|instance_eval$)/
      undef_method name
    end
  end
  # ...

  instance_methods.each { |m| hide(m) }
end
```

Builder doesn't go as far as removing each and every method from BlankSlate. It keeps instance_eval (a method that you'll get to know in the next chapter) and all the "reserved methods"—methods that are used internally by Ruby, whose names conventionally begin with a double underscore. One example of a reserved method is BasicObject#_send_, which behaves the same as send but gives you a scary warning when you try to remove it. The case of instance_eval is more of a judgement call: you could choose to remove it, but Builder decided not to.

Now that you know about Blank Slates, you can finally fix the bug in the Computer class.

Fixing the Computer Class

To turn Computer into a *Blank Slate (66)* and fix the display method bug, you and Bill make it a subclass of BasicObject:

➤ ```
class Computer < BasicObject
  # ...
```

There is one last improvement you can make to this class. BasicObject doesn't have a respond_to? method. (respond_to? is a method of BasicObject's subclass Object.) Because you don't have respond_to?, you can delete the now pointless respond_to_missing? method that you and Bill added back in *respond_to_missing?*, on page 62. Once you do that, you're finally done with the method_missing-based implementation of Computer.

## Wrap-Up

Let's review today's work. You and Bill started with a Computer class that contained lots of duplication. (The original class is in *Double, Treble... Trouble*, on page 47.) You removed the duplication in two different ways.

Your first attempt relied on *Dynamic Methods (51)* and *Dynamic Dispatch (48)*:

**methods/computer/more_dynamic_methods.rb**
```ruby
class Computer
  def initialize(computer_id, data_source)
    @id = computer_id
    @data_source = data_source
    data_source.methods.grep(/^get_(.*)_info$/) { Computer.define_component $1 }
  end

  def self.define_component(name)
    define_method(name) do
      info = @data_source.send "get_#{name}_info", @id
      price = @data_source.send "get_#{name}_price", @id
      result = "#{name.capitalize}: #{info} ($#{price})"
      return "* #{result}" if price >= 100
      result
    end
  end
end
```
```

Your second attempt centered around *Ghost Methods (57)* (to be more precise, it used a *Dynamic Proxy (60)* that is also a *Blank Slate (66)*):

```
methods/computer/blank_slate.rb
class Computer < BasicObject
  def initialize(computer_id, data_source)
    @id = computer_id
    @data_source = data_source
  end

  def method_missing(name, *args)
    super if !@data_source.respond_to?("get_#{name}_info")
    info = @data_source.send("get_#{name}_info", @id)
    price = @data_source.send("get_#{name}_price", @id)
    result = "#{name.capitalize}: #{info} ($#{price})"
    return "* #{result}" if price >= 100
    result
  end
end
```

Neither solution would be practical without Ruby's dynamic capabilities. If you come from a static language, you're probably accustomed to spotting and removing duplication *inside* your methods. In Ruby, you might want to look for duplication *among* methods as well. Then you can remove that duplication with some of the spells you've learned today.

You and Bill can consider the two solutions. It's time to make a choice. Which one do you like best?

Dynamic Methods vs. Ghost Methods

As you experienced yourself, *Ghost Methods (57)* can be dangerous. You can avoid most of their problems by following a few basic recommendations (always call super, always redefine respond_to_missing?)—but even then, Ghost Methods can sometimes cause puzzling bugs.[2]

The problems with Ghost Methods boil down to the fact that they are not really methods; instead, they're just a way to intercept method calls. Because of this, they behave differently from actual methods. For example, they don't appear in the list of names returned by Object#methods. In contrast, Dynamic Methods are just regular methods that happened to be defined with define_method instead of def, and they behave the same as any other method.

---

2. A presentation on the perils of method_missing is at http://www.everytalk.tv/talks/1881-Madison-Ruby-The-Revenge-of-method-missing.

There are times when Ghost Methods are your only viable option. This usually happens when you have a large number of method calls, or when you don't know what method calls you might need at runtime. For an example, look back at the Builder library in *The Builder Example*, on page 67. Builder couldn't define a Dynamic Method for each of the potentially infinite XML tags that you might want to generate, so it uses method_missing to intercept method calls instead.

All things considered, the choice between Dynamic and Ghost Methods depends on your experience and coding style, but you can follow a simple rule of thumb when in doubt: *use Dynamic Methods if you can and Ghost Methods if you have to.*

You and Bill decide to follow this rule, and you commit the define_method-based version of Computer to the project repository. Tomorrow is sure to be another day of coding challenges, so it's time to head home and rest up.

Wednesday: Blocks

Yesterday you learned a lot about methods and method calls. Today you will deal with *blocks*.

You're probably already familiar with blocks—you can't write much Ruby code without them. But what you might not know is that blocks are a powerful tool for controlling *scope*, meaning which variables and methods can be seen by which lines of code. In this chapter, you'll discover how this control of scope makes blocks a cornerstone of Ruby metaprogramming.

Blocks are just one member of a larger family of "callable objects," which include objects such as procs and lambdas. This chapter shows how you can use these and other callable objects to their greatest advantage—for example, to store a block and execute it later.

Just a short public service announcement before getting started: the previous chapters never strayed far from the usual object-oriented concepts, such as classes, objects, and methods. Blocks have a different heritage that can be traced back to functional programming languages, such as LISP. If you think in objects and classes, expect to deal with some novel concepts in this chapter. You're likely to find these concepts strange and, at the same time, fascinating.

With that sneak peek into what this chapter is all about, it's now time to step into the office.

The Day of the Blocks

Where you and Bill agree to put off today's job, make a roadmap, and review the basics of blocks.

You've barely had time to check your mail, and Bill is already making his way to your desk, eager to get to work. "I talked with the boss about today's job," he says. "I won't go into the details now, but I can tell you that we're going to need *blocks* for today's project." Before the two of you jump into the fray, you need to understand the nuances of blocks. You agree to spend the morning talking about blocks, putting off today's project until after lunch.

Today's Roadmap

On a sheet of paper, Bill lists the things he wants to cover:

- A review of the basics of blocks

- An overview of *scopes* and how you can carry variables through scopes by using blocks as *closures*

- How you can further manipulate scopes by passing a block to instance_eval

- How you can convert blocks into *callable objects* that you can set aside and call later, such as Procs and lambdas

You start with the first point—a quick review of the basics. (If you already know the basics of Ruby blocks, you can skip straight to *Blocks Are Closures*, on page 77.)

The Basics of Blocks

Do you remember how blocks work? Here is a simple example to refresh your memory:

blocks/basics_failure.rb

```
def a_method(a, b)
  a + yield(a, b)
end

a_method(1, 2) {|x, y| (x + y) * 3 }   # => 10
```

You can define a block with either curly braces or the do...end keywords. A common convention is to use curly braces for single-line blocks and do...end for multiline blocks.

You can define a block only when you call a method. The block is passed straight into the method, and the method can call back to the block with the yield keyword.

Optionally, a block can have arguments, like x and y in the previous example. When you yield to the block, you can provide values for its arguments, just like you do when you call a method. Also, like a method, a block returns the result of the last line of code it evaluates.

Within a method, you can ask Ruby whether the current call includes a block. You can do that with the Kernel#block_given? method:

```ruby
def a_method
  return yield if block_given?
  'no block'
end

a_method                        # => "no block"
a_method { "here's a block!" }  # => "here's a block!"
```

If you use yield when block_given? is false, you'll get a runtime error.

Now you can apply what you know about blocks to a real-life scenario.

Quiz: Ruby#

Where you're challenged to do something useful with blocks.

Bill shares a little secret: "You know, a few years ago I was making a living out of writing C# code. I must admit that C# did have a few nice features. Let me show you one of those."

The using Keyword

Imagine that you're writing a C# program that connects to a remote server and you have an object that represents the connection:

```csharp
RemoteConnection conn = new RemoteConnection("my_server");
String stuff = conn.ReadStuff();
conn.Dispose();    // close the connection to avoid a leak
```

This code correctly disposes of the connection after using it. However, it doesn't deal with exceptions. If ReadStuff throws an exception, then the last line is never executed, and conn is never disposed of. What the code *should* do is manage exceptions, disposing of the connection regardless of whether an exception is thrown. C# provides a keyword named using that goes through the whole process for you:

```csharp
RemoteConnection conn = new RemoteConnection("some_remote_server");
using (conn)
{
    conn.ReadData();
    DoMoreStuff();
}
```

The using keyword expects that conn has a method named Dispose. This method is called automatically after the code in the curly braces, regardless of whether an exception is thrown.

The Challenge

To refresh the basics of blocks, Bill throws a challenge at you: write a Ruby version of using. Instead of calling it using, call it with, because using is already a keyword in Ruby. Use this test to make sure that your with works like C#'s using:

blocks/with_test.rb

```ruby
require 'test/unit'
require_relative 'with'

class TestWith < Test::Unit::TestCase
  class Resource
    def dispose
      @disposed = true
    end

    def disposed?
      @disposed
    end
  end

  def test_disposes_of_resources
    r = Resource.new
    with(r) {}
    assert r.disposed?
  end

  def test_disposes_of_resources_in_case_of_exception
    r = Resource.new
    assert_raises(Exception) {
      with(r) {
        raise Exception
      }
    }
    assert r.disposed?
  end
end
```

Quiz Solution

Take a look at this solution to the quiz:

blocks/with.rb

```ruby
module Kernel
  def with(resource)
    begin
      yield
    ensure
      resource.dispose
    end
```

```
      end
end
```

You can't define a new keyword, but you can fake it with a *Kernel Method (32)*. Kernel#with takes the managed resource as an argument. It also takes a block, which it executes. Regardless of whether the block completes normally, the ensure clause calls dispose on the resource to release it cleanly. There is no rescue clause, so any exception is still propagated to the code that calls Kernel#with.

Now that you've reviewed block basics, you can move to the second item on the list from *Today's Roadmap*, on page 74: closures.

Blocks Are Closures

Where you find there is more to blocks than meets the eye and you learn how to smuggle variables across scopes.

As Bill notes on a piece of scratch paper, a block is not just a floating piece of code. You can't run code in a vacuum. When code runs, it needs an *environment*: local variables, instance variables, self....

Because these entities are basically names bound to objects, you can call them the *bindings* for short. The main point about blocks is that they are all inclusive and come ready to run. They contain both the code *and* a set of bindings.

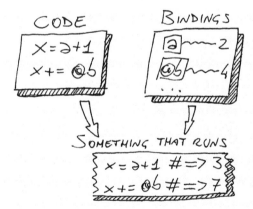

You're probably wondering where the block picks up its bindings. When you define the block, it simply grabs the bindings that are there at that moment, and then it carries those bindings along when you pass the block into a method:

blocks/blocks_and_bindings.rb

```ruby
def my_method
  x = "Goodbye"
  yield("cruel")
end

x = "Hello"
my_method {|y| "#{x}, #{y} world" } # => "Hello, cruel world"
```

When you create the block, you capture the local bindings, such as x. Then you pass the block to a method that has its own separate set of bindings. In the previous example, those bindings also include a variable named x. Still, the code in the block sees the x that was around when the block was defined, not the method's x, which is not visible at all in the block.

You can also define additional bindings inside the block, but they disappear after the block ends:

blocks/block_local_vars_failure.rb

```ruby
def just_yield
  yield
end

top_level_variable = 1

just_yield do
  top_level_variable += 1
  local_to_block = 1
end

top_level_variable  # => 2
local_to_block      # => Error!
```

Because of the properties above, a computer scientist would say that a block is a *closure*. For the rest of us, this means a block captures the local bindings and carries them along with it.

So, how do you use closures in practice? To understand that, take a closer look at the place where all the bindings reside—the *scope*. Here you'll learn to identify the spots where a program changes scope, and you'll encounter a particular problem with changing scopes that can be solved with closures.

Scope

Imagine being a little debugger making your way through a Ruby program. You jump from statement to statement until you finally hit a breakpoint. Now catch your breath and look around. See the scenery around you? That's your *scope*.

You can see bindings all over the scope. Look down at your feet, and you see a bunch of local variables. Raise your head, and you see that you're standing within an object, with its own methods and instance variables; that's the current object, also known as self. Farther away, you see the tree of constants so clear that you could mark your current position on a map. Squint your eyes, and you can even see a bunch of global variables off in the distance.

But what happens when you get tired of the scenery and decide to move on?

Changing Scope

This example shows how scope changes as your program runs, tracking the names of bindings with the Kernel#local_variables method:

blocks/scopes.rb

```
v1 = 1
class MyClass
  v2 = 2
  local_variables      # => [:v2]
  def my_method
    v3 = 3
    local_variables
  end
  local_variables      # => [:v2]
end

obj = MyClass.new
obj.my_method          # => [:v3]
obj.my_method          # => [:v3]
local_variables        # => [:v1, :obj]
```

Track the program as it moves through scopes. It starts within the top-level scope that you read about in *The Top Level*, on page 34. After defining v1 in the top-level scope, the program enters the scope of MyClass's definition. What happens then?

Some languages, such as Java and C#, allow "inner scopes" to see variables from "outer scopes." That kind of nested visibility doesn't happen in Ruby, where scopes are sharply separated: as soon as you enter a new scope, the previous bindings are replaced by a new set of bindings. This means that when the program enters MyClass, v1 "falls out of scope" and is no longer visible.

In the scope of the definition of MyClass, the program defines v2 and a method. The code in the method isn't executed yet, so the program never opens a new scope until the end of the class definition. There, the scope opened with the class keyword is closed, and the program gets back to the top-level scope.

Global Variables and Top-Level Instance Variables

Global variables can be accessed by any scope:

```ruby
def a_scope
  $var = "some value"
end

def another_scope
  $var
end

a_scope
another_scope # => "some value"
```

The problem with global variables is that every part of the system can change them, so in no time you'll find it difficult to track who is changing what. For this reason, the general rule is this: when it comes to global variables, use them sparingly, if ever.

You can sometimes use a top-level instance variable in place of a global variable. These are the instance variables of the top-level main object, described in *The Top Level*, on page 34:

```ruby
@var = "The top-level @var"

def my_method
  @var
end

my_method # => "The top-level @var"
```

You can access a top-level instance variable whenever main takes the role of self, as in the previous example. When any other object is self, the top-level instance variable is out of scope.

```ruby
class MyClass
  def my_method
    @var = "This is not the top-level @var!"
  end
end
```

Being less universally accessible, top-level instance variables are generally considered safer than global variables—but not by a wide margin.

What happens when the program creates a MyClass object and calls my_method twice? The first time the program enters my_method, it opens a new scope and defines a local variable, v3. Then the program exits the method, falling back to the top-level scope. At this point, the method's scope is lost. When the program calls my_method a second time, it opens yet another new scope, and it defines a new v3 variable (unrelated to the previous v3, which is now lost). Finally, the program returns to the top-level scope, where you can see v1 and obj again. Phew!

Here is the example's important point: "Whenever the program changes scope, some bindings are replaced by a new set of bindings." Granted, this doesn't happen to all the bindings each and every time. For example, if a method calls another method on the same object, instance variables stay in scope through the call. In general, though, bindings tend to fall out of scope when the scope changes. In particular, local variables change at every new scope. (That's why they're "local.")

As you can see, keeping track of scopes can be a tricky task. You can spot scopes more quickly if you learn about *Scope Gates*.

Scope Gates

There are exactly three places where a program leaves the previous scope behind and opens a new one:

- Class definitions
- Module definitions
- Methods

Scope changes whenever the program enters (or exits) a class or module definition or a method. These three borders are marked by the keywords class, module, and def, respectively. Each of these keywords acts like a *Scope Gate*.

Spell: Scope Gate, page 241

For example, here is the previous example program again, with Scope Gates clearly marked by comments:

```
v1 = 1
class MyClass        # SCOPE GATE: entering class
  v2 = 2
  local_variables    # => ["v2"]
  def my_method      # SCOPE GATE: entering def
    v3 = 3
    local_variables
  end                # SCOPE GATE: leaving def
  local_variables    # => ["v2"]
end                  # SCOPE GATE: leaving class
obj = MyClass.new
obj.my_method        # => [:v3]
local_variables      # => [:v1, :obj]
```

Now it's easy to see that this program opens three separate scopes: the top-level scope, one new scope when it enters MyClass, and one new scope when it calls my_method.

There is a subtle difference between class and module on one side and def on the other. The code in a class or module definition is executed immediately.

Conversely, the code in a method definition is executed later, when you eventually call the method. However, as you write your program, you usually don't care *when* it changes scope—you only care that it does.

Now you can pinpoint the places where your program changes scope—the spots marked by class, module, and def. But what if you want to pass a variable through one of these spots? This question takes you back to blocks.

Flattening the Scope

The more you become proficient in Ruby, the more you get into difficult situations where you want to pass bindings through a *Scope Gate (81)*:

blocks/flat_scope_1.rb

```ruby
my_var = "Success"

class MyClass
  # We want to print my_var here...

  def my_method
    #  ..and here
  end
end
```

Scope Gates are quite a formidable barrier. As soon as you walk through one of them, local variables fall out of scope. So, how can you carry my_var across not one but two Scope Gates?

Look at the class Scope Gate first. You can't pass my_var through it, but you can replace class with something else that is not a Scope Gate: a method call. If you could call a method instead of using the class keyword, you could capture my_var in a closure and pass that closure to the method. Can you think of a method that does the same thing that class does?

If you look at Ruby's documentation, you'll find the answer: Class.new is a perfect replacement for class. You can also define instance methods in the class if you pass a block to Class.new:

blocks/flat_scope_2.rb

```ruby
my_var = "Success"
➤ MyClass = Class.new do
➤   # Now we can print my_var here...
➤   puts "#{my_var} in the class definition!"

  def my_method
    # ...but how can we print it here?
  end
end
```

Now, how can you pass my_var through the def Scope Gate? Once again, you have to replace the keyword with a method call. Think of the discussion about *Dynamic Methods (51)*: instead of def, you can use Module#define_method:

blocks/flat_scope_3.rb

```
my_var = "Success"

MyClass = Class.new do
  puts "#{my_var} in the class definition"

➤  define_method :my_method do
➤    puts "#{my_var} in the method"
➤  end
end

➤ MyClass.new.my_method

❮ Success in the class definition
  Success in the method
```

If you replace Scope Gates with method calls, you allow one scope to see variables from another scope. Technically, this trick should be called *nested lexical scopes*, but many Ruby coders refer to it simply as "flattening the scope," meaning that the two scopes share variables as if the scopes were squeezed together. For short, you can call this spell a *Flat Scope*.

Spell: Flat Scope, page 236

Sharing the Scope

Once you know about *Flat Scopes (83)*, you can do pretty much whatever you want with scopes. For example, maybe you want to share a variable among a few methods, and you don't want anybody else to see that variable. You can do that by defining all the methods in the same Flat Scope as the variable:

blocks/shared_scope.rb

```
def define_methods
  shared = 0

  Kernel.send :define_method, :counter do
    shared
  end
  Kernel.send :define_method, :inc do |x|
    shared += x
  end
end

define_methods

counter        # => 0
inc(4)
counter        # => 4
```

This example defines two *Kernel Methods (32)*. (It also uses *Dynamic Dispatch (48)* to access the private class method define_method on Kernel.) Both Kernel#counter and Kernel#inc can see the shared variable. No other method can see shared, because it's protected by a *Scope Gate (81)*—that's what the define_methods method is for. This smart way to control the sharing of variables is called a *Shared Scope*.

Spell: Shared Scope, page 241

Shared Scopes are not used much in practice, but they're a powerful trick and a good example of the power of scopes. With a combination of Scope Gates, Flat Scopes, and Shared Scopes, you can twist and bend your scopes to see exactly the variables you need, from the place you want. Now that you wield this power, it's time for a wrap-up of Ruby closures.

Closures Wrap-Up

Each Ruby scope contains a bunch of bindings, and the scopes are separated by *Scope Gates (81)*: class, module, and def.

If you want to sneak a binding or two through a Scope Gate, you can use blocks. A block is a *closure*: when you define a block, it captures the bindings in the current environment and carries them around. So you can replace the Scope Gate with a method call, capture the current bindings in a closure, and pass the closure to the method.

You can replace class with Class.new, module with Module.new, and def with Module#define_method. This is a *Flat Scope (83)*, the basic closure-related spell.

If you define multiple methods in the same Flat Scope, maybe protected by a Scope Gate, they all can share bindings. That's called a *Shared Scope (84)*.

Bill glances at the road map he created. (See *Today's Roadmap*, on page 74.) "Now that you've gotten a taste of Flat Scopes, we should move on to something more advanced: instance_eval."

instance_eval()

Where you learn another way to mix code and bindings at will.

The following program demonstrates BasicObject#instance_eval, which evaluates a block in the context of an object:

```
blocks/instance_eval.rb
class MyClass
  def initialize
    @v = 1
  end
```

```
end
obj = MyClass.new
obj.instance_eval do
  self          # => #<MyClass:0x3340dc @v=1>
  @v            # => 1
end
```

The block is evaluated with the receiver as self, so it can access the receiver's private methods and instance variables, such as @v. Even if instance_eval changes self, the block that you pass to instance_eval can still see the bindings from the place where it's defined, like any other block:

```
v = 2
obj.instance_eval { @v = v }
obj.instance_eval { @v }        # => 2
```

The three lines in the previous example are evaluated in the same *Flat Scope (83)*, so they can all access the local variable v—but the blocks are evaluated with the object as self, so they can also access obj's instance variable @v. In all these cases, you can call the block that you pass to instance_eval a *Context Probe*, because it's like a snippet of code that you dip inside an object to do something in there.

Spell: Context Probe, page 234

Breaking Encapsulation

At this point, you might be horrified. With a *Context Probe (85)*, you can wreak havoc on encapsulation! No data is private data anymore. Isn't that a Very Bad Thing?

Pragmatically, there are some situations where encapsulation just gets in your way. For one, you might want to take a quick peek inside an object from an irb command line. In a case like this, breaking into the object with instance_eval is often the shortest route.

Another acceptable reason to break encapsulation is arguably testing. Here's an example.

The Padrino Example

The Padrino web framework defines a Logger class that manages all the logging that a web application must deal with. The Logger stores its own configuration into instance variables. For example, @log_static is true if the application must log access to static files.

Padrino's unit tests need to change the configuration of the application's logger. Instead of going through the trouble of creating and configuring a new logger, the following tests (written with the minitest gem) just pry open the existing application logger and change its configuration with a Context Probe:

gems/padrino-core-0.11.3/test/test_logger.rb

```ruby
describe "PadrinoLogger" do
  context 'for logger functionality' do
    context "static asset logging" do
      should 'not log static assets by default' do
        # ...
        get "/images/something.png"
        assert_equal "Foo", body
        assert_match "", Padrino.logger.log.string
      end

      should 'allow turning on static assets logging' do
        Padrino.logger.instance_eval{ @log_static = true }
        # ...
        get "/images/something.png"
        assert_equal "Foo", body
        assert_match /GET/, Padrino.logger.log.string
        Padrino.logger.instance_eval{ @log_static = false }
      end
    end

    # ...
```

The first test accesses a static file and checks that the logger doesn't log anything. This is Padrino's default behavior. The second test uses instance_eval to change the logger's configuration and enable static file logging. Then it accesses the same URL as the first test and checks that the logger actually logged something. Before exiting, the second test resets static file logging to the default false state.

You can easily criticize these tests for being fragile: if the implementation of Logger changes and the @log_static instance variable disappears, then the test will break. Like many other things in Ruby, encapsulation is a flexible tool that you can choose to ignore, and it's up to you to decide if and when to accept that risk. The authors of Padrino decided that a quick hack inside the logger object was an acceptable workaround in this case.

instance_exec()

instance_eval has a slightly more flexible twin brother named instance_exec that allows you to pass arguments to the block. This feature is useful in a few rare cases, such as the one in this artfully complicated example:

blocks/instance_exec.rb

```
class C
  def initialize
    @x = 1
  end
end

class D
  def twisted_method
    @y = 2
    C.new.instance_eval { "@x: #{@x}, @y: #{@y}" }
  end
end

D.new.twisted_method   # => "@x: 1, @y: "
```

You might assume that the block in D#twisted_method can access both the @x instance variable from C and the @y instance variable from D in the same *Flat Scope (83)*. However, instance variables depend on self, so when instance_eval switches self to the receiver, all the instance variables in the caller fall out of scope. The code inside the block interprets @y as an instance variable of C that hasn't been initialized, and as such is nil (and prints out as an empty string).

To merge @x and @y in the same scope, you can use instance_exec to pass @y's value to the block:

```
class D
  def twisted_method
    @y = 2
➤    C.new.instance_exec(@y) {|y| "@x: #{@x}, @y: #{y}" }
  end
end

D.new.twisted_method   # => "@x: 1, @y: 2"
```

Clean Rooms

Sometimes you create an object just to evaluate blocks inside it. An object like that can be called a *Clean Room*:

Spell: Clean Room, page 233

blocks/clean_room.rb

```
class CleanRoom
  def current_temperature
    # ...
  end
end


clean_room = CleanRoom.new
clean_room.instance_eval do
```

```ruby
  if current_temperature < 20
    # TODO: wear jacket
  end
end
```

A Clean Room is just an environment where you can evaluate your blocks. It can expose a few useful methods that the block can call, such as current_temperature in the example above. However, the ideal Clean Room doesn't have many methods or instance variables, because the names of those methods and instance variables could clash with the names in the environment that the block comes from. For this reason, instances of BasicObject usually make for good Clean Rooms, because they're *Blank Slates (66)*—so they barely have any method at all.

(Interestingly, BasicObject is even cleaner than that: in a BasicObject, standard Ruby constants such as String are out of scope. If you want to reference a constant from a BasicObject, you have to use its absolute path, such as ::String.)

You'll find a practical example of a Clean Room in *Quiz: A Better DSL*, on page 98.

That's all you have to know about instance_eval. Now you can move on to the last topic in today's roadmap: callable objects.

Callable Objects

Where you learn how blocks are just part of a larger family, and Bill shows you how to set code aside and execute it later.

If you get to the bottom of it, using a block is a two-step process. First, you set some code aside, and second, you call the block (with yield) to execute the code. This "package code first, call it later" mechanism is not exclusive to blocks. There are at least three other places in Ruby where you can package code:

- In a *proc*, which is basically a block turned object
- In a *lambda*, which is a slight variation on a proc
- In a *method*

Procs and lambdas are the big ones to talk about here. We'll start with them and bring methods back into the picture later.

Proc Objects

Although most things in Ruby are objects, blocks are not. But why would you care about that? Imagine that you want to store a block and execute it later. To do that, you need an object.

To solve this problem, Ruby provides the standard library class Proc. A Proc is a block that has been turned into an object. You can create a Proc by passing the block to Proc.new. Later, you can evaluate the block-turned-object with Proc#call:

```
inc = Proc.new {|x| x + 1 }
# more code...
inc.call(2) # => 3
```

This technique is called a *Deferred Evaluation*.

Spell: Deferred Evaluation, page 234

There are a few more ways to create Procs in Ruby. Ruby provides two *Kernel Methods (32)* that convert a block to a Proc: lambda and proc. In a short while, you'll see that there are subtle differences between creating Procs with lambda and creating them in any other way, but in most cases you can just use whichever one you like best:

```
dec = lambda {|x| x - 1 }
dec.class # => Proc
dec.call(2) # => 1
```

Also, you can create a lambda with the so-called "stabby lambda" operator:

```
p = ->(x) { x + 1 }
```

Notice the little arrow. The previous code is the same as the following:

```
p = lambda {|x| x + 1 }
```

So far, you have seen not one, but four different ways to convert a block to a Proc. There is also a fifth way, which deserves its own section.

The & Operator

A block is like an additional, anonymous argument to a method. In most cases, you execute the block right there in the method, using yield. In two cases, yield is not enough:

- You want to pass the block to another method (or even another block).
- You want to convert the block to a Proc.

In both cases, you need to point at the block and say, "I want to use *this* block"—to do that, you need a name. To attach a binding to the block, you can add one special argument to the method. This argument must be the last in the list of arguments and prefixed by an & sign. Here's a method that passes the block to another method:

blocks/ampersand.rb

```ruby
def math(a, b)
  yield(a, b)
end

def do_math(a, b, &operation)
  math(a, b, &operation)
end

do_math(2, 3) {|x, y| x * y}  # => 6
```

If you call do_math without a block, the &operation argument is bound to nil, and the yield operation in math fails.

What if you want to convert the block to a Proc? As it turns out, if you referenced operation in the previous code, you'd already have a Proc object. The real meaning of the & is this: "I want to take the block that is passed to this method and turn it into a Proc." Just drop the &, and you'll be left with a Proc again:

```ruby
def my_method(&the_proc)
  the_proc
end

p = my_method {|name| "Hello, #{name}!" }
p.class          # => Proc
p.call("Bill")   # => "Hello, Bill!"
```

You now know a bunch of different ways to convert a block to a Proc. But what if you want to convert it back? Again, you can use the & modifier to convert the Proc to a block:

blocks/proc_to_block.rb

```ruby
def my_method(greeting)
  "#{greeting}, #{yield}!"
end

my_proc = proc { "Bill" }
my_method("Hello", &my_proc)
```

When you call my_method, the & converts my_proc to a block and passes that block to the method.

Now you know how to convert a block to a Proc and back again. Let's look at a real-life example of a callable object that starts its life as a lambda and is then converted to a regular block.

The HighLine Example

The HighLine gem helps you automate console input and output. For example, you can tell HighLine to collect comma-separated user input and split it into an array, all in a single call. Here's a Ruby program that lets you input a comma-separated list of friends:

blocks/highline_example.rb

```
require 'highline'

hl = HighLine.new
friends = hl.ask("Friends?", lambda {|s| s.split(',') })
puts "You're friends with: #{friends.inspect}"
```

❮ Friends?
⇒ **Ivana, Roberto, Olaf**
❮ You're friends with: ["Ivana", " Roberto", " Olaf"]

You call HighLine#ask with a string (the question for the user) and a Proc that contains the post-processing code. (You might wonder why HighLine requires a Proc argument rather than a simple block. Actually, you *can* pass a block to ask, but that mechanism is reserved for a different HighLine feature.)

If you read the code of HighLine#ask, you'll see that it passes the Proc to an object of class Question, which stores the Proc as an instance variable. Later, after collecting the user's input, the Question passes the input to the stored Proc.

If you want to do something else to the user's input—say, change it to uppercase—you just create a different Proc:

```
name = hl.ask("Name?", lambda {|s| s.capitalize })
puts "Hello, #{name}"
```

❮ Name?
⇒ **bill**
❮ Hello, Bill

This is an example of *Deferred Evaluation (89)*.

Procs vs. Lambdas

You've learned a bunch of different ways to turn a block into a Proc: Proc.new, lambda, the & modifier.... In all cases, the resulting object is a Proc.

Confusingly, though, Procs created with lambda differ in some respects from Procs created any other way. The differences are subtle but important enough that people refer to the two kinds of Procs by distinct names: Procs created with lambda are called *lambdas*, while the others are simply *procs*. (You can use the Proc#lambda? method to check whether the Proc is a lambda.)

One word of warning before you dive into this section: the difference between procs and lambdas is probably the most confusing feature of Ruby, with lots of special cases and arbitrary distinctions. There's no need to go into all the gory details, but you need to know, at least roughly, the important differences.

There are two differences between procs and lambdas. One has to do with the return keyword, and the other concerns the checking of arguments. Let's start with return.

Procs, Lambdas, and return

The first difference between lambdas and procs is that the return keyword means different things. In a lambda, return just returns from the lambda:

blocks/proc_vs_lambda.rb
```ruby
def double(callable_object)
  callable_object.call * 2
end

l = lambda { return 10 }
double(l) # => 20
```

In a proc, return behaves differently. Rather than return from the proc, it returns from the scope where the proc itself was defined:

```ruby
def another_double
  p = Proc.new { return 10 }
  result = p.call
  return result * 2  # unreachable code!
end

another_double # => 10
```

If you're aware of this behavior, you can steer clear of buggy code like this:

```ruby
def double(callable_object)
  callable_object.call * 2
end

p = Proc.new { return 10 }
double(p)     # => LocalJumpError
```

The previous program tries to return from the scope where p is defined. Because you can't return from the top-level scope, the program fails. You can avoid this kind of mistake if you avoid using explicit returns:

```ruby
p = Proc.new { 10 }
double(p)    # => 20
```

Now on to the second important difference between procs and lambdas.

Procs, Lambdas, and Arity

The second difference between procs and lambdas concerns the way they check their arguments. For example, a particular proc or lambda might have an *arity* of two, meaning that it accepts two arguments:

```
p = Proc.new {|a, b| [a, b]}
p.arity # => 2
```

What happens if you call this callable object with three arguments, or one single argument? The long answer to this question is complicated and littered with special cases.[1] The short answer is that, in general, lambdas tend to be less tolerant than procs (and regular blocks) when it comes to arguments. Call a lambda with the wrong arity, and it fails with an ArgumentError. On the other hand, a proc fits the argument list to its own expectations:

```
p = Proc.new {|a, b| [a, b]}
p.call(1, 2, 3)    # => [1, 2]
p.call(1)          # => [1, nil]
```

If there are too many arguments, a proc drops the excess arguments. If there are too few arguments, it assigns nil to the missing arguments.

Procs vs. Lambdas: The Verdict

You now know the differences between procs and lambdas. But you're wondering which kind of Proc you should use in your own code.

Generally speaking, lambdas are more intuitive than procs because they're more similar to methods. They're pretty strict about arity, and they simply exit when you call return. For this reason, many Rubyists use lambdas as a first choice, unless they need the specific features of procs.

Method Objects

For the sake of completeness, you might want to take one more look at the last member of the callable objects' family: methods. If you're not convinced that methods, like lambdas, are just callable objects, look at this code:

blocks/methods.rb

```
class MyClass
  def initialize(value)
    @x = value
  end
```

---

1. A program to explore those special cases, written by Paul Cantrell, is at http://innig.net/software/ruby/closures-in-ruby.rb.

```
  def my_method
    @x
  end
end

object = MyClass.new(1)
m = object.method :my_method
m.call                              # => 1
```

By calling Kernel#method, you get the method itself as a Method object, which you can later execute with Method#call. In Ruby 2.1, you also have Kernel#singleton_method, which converts the name of a *Singleton Method (115)* to a Method object. (What are you saying? You don't know what a Singleton Method is yet? Oh, you will, you will…)

A Method object is similar to a block or a lambda. Indeed, you can convert a Method to a Proc by calling Method#to_proc, and you can convert a block to a method with define_method. However, an important difference exists between lambdas and methods: a lambda is evaluated in the scope it's defined in (it's a closure, remember?), while a Method is evaluated in the scope of its object.

Ruby has a second class that represents methods—one you might find perplexing. Let's have a look at it first, and then we'll see how it can be used.

Unbound Methods

UnboundMethods are like Methods that have been detached from their original class or module. You can turn a Method into an UnboundMethod by calling Method#unbind. You can also get an UnboundMethod directly by calling Module#instance_method, as in the following example:

```
blocks/unbound_methods.rb
```

```
module MyModule
  def my_method
    42
  end
end

unbound = MyModule.instance_method(:my_method)
unbound.class                    # => UnboundMethod
```

You can't call an UnboundMethod, but you can use it to generate a normal method that you can call. You do that by binding the UnboundMethod to an object with UnboundMethod#bind. UnboundMethods that come from a class can only be bound to objects of the same class (or a subclass), while UnboundMethods that come from a module have no such limitation from Ruby 2.0 onward. You can also bind an UnboundMethod by passing it to Module#define_method:

```
String.send :define_method, :another_method, unbound

"abc".another_method  # => 42
```

(I used a *Dynamic Dispatch (48)* to call define_method on String, because it's a private method.)

UnboundMethods are used only in very special cases. Let's look at one of those.

The Active Support Example

The Active Support gem contains, among other utilities, a set of classes and modules that automatically load a Ruby file when you use a constant defined in that file. This "autoloading" system includes a module named Loadable that redefines the standard Kernel#load method. If a class includes Loadable, then Loadable#load gets lower than Kernel#load on its chain of ancestors—so a call to load will end up in Loadable#load.

In some cases, you might want to remove autoloading from a class that has already included Loadable. In other words, you want to stop using Loadable#load and go back to the plain vanilla Kernel#load. Ruby has no uninclude method, so you cannot remove Loadable from your ancestors once you have included it. Active Support works around this problem with a single line of code:

gems/activesupport-4.1.0/lib/active_support/dependencies.rb

```
module Loadable
  def self.exclude_from(base)
    base.class_eval { define_method(:load, Kernel.instance_method(:load)) }
  end

  # ...
```

Imagine that you have a MyClass class that includes Loadable. When you call Loadable.exclude_from(MyClass), the code above calls instance_method to get the original Kernel#load as an UnboundMethod. Then it uses that UnboundMethod to define a brand-new load method directly on MyClass. As a result, MyClass#load is actually the same method as Kernel#load, and it overrides the load method in Loadable. (If that sounds confusing, try drawing a picture of MyClass's ancestors chain, and everything will be clear.)

This trick is an example of the power of UnboundMethods, but it's also a contrived solution to a very specific problem—a solution that leaves you with a confusing chain of ancestors that contains three load methods, two of which are identical to each other (Kernel#load and MyClass#load), and two of which are never called (Kernel#load and Loadable#load). It's probably good policy not to try this kind of class hacking at home.

Callable Objects Wrap-Up

Callable objects are snippets of code that you can evaluate, and they carry their own scope along with them. They can be the following:

- *Blocks* (they aren't really "objects," but they are still "callable"): Evaluated in the scope in which they're defined.

- *Procs*: Objects of class Proc. Like blocks, they are evaluated in the scope where they're defined.

- *Lambdas*: Also objects of class Proc but subtly different from regular procs. They're closures like blocks and procs, and as such they're evaluated in the scope where they're defined.

- *Methods*: Bound to an object, they are evaluated in that object's scope. They can also be rebound to a different object or class.

Different callable objects exhibit subtly different behaviors. In methods and lambdas, return returns from the callable object, while in procs and blocks, return returns from the callable object's original context. Different callable objects also react differently to calls with the wrong arity. Methods are stricter, lambdas are almost as strict (save for some corner cases), and procs and blocks are more tolerant.

These differences notwithstanding, you can still convert from one callable object to another, such as by using Proc.new, Method#to_proc, or the & modifier.

Writing a Domain-Specific Language

Where you and Bill, at long last, write some code.

"Enough talking about blocks," Bill says. "It's time to focus on today's job. Let's call it the RedFlag project."

RedFlag is a monitor utility for the people in the sales department. It should send the sales folks a message when an order is late, when total sales are too low...basically, whenever one of many different things happens. Sales wants to monitor dozens of different events, and the list is bound to change every week or so.

Luckily for you and Bill, sales has full-time programmers, so you don't have to write the events yourself. You can just write a simple Domain-Specific Language. (You can read about DSLs in Appendix 2, *Domain-Specific Languages*, on page 227.) The sales guys can then use this DSL to define events, like this:

```
event "we're earning wads of money" do
  recent_orders = ...   # (read from database)
  recent_orders > 1000
end
```

To define an event, you give it a description and a block of code. If the block returns true, then you get an alert via mail. If it returns false, then nothing happens. The system should check all the events every few minutes.

It's time to write RedFlag 0.1.

Your First DSL

You and Bill put together a working RedFlag DSL in no time:

blocks/redflag_1/redflag.rb

```
def event(description)
  puts "ALERT: #{description}" if yield
end
load 'events.rb'
```

The entire DSL is just one method and a line that executes a file named events.rb. The code in events.rb is supposed to call back into RedFlag's event method. To test the DSL, you create a quick events file:

blocks/redflag_1/events.rb

```
event "an event that always happens" do
  true
end
event "an event that never happens" do
  false
end
```

You save both redflag.rb and events.rb in the same folder and run redflag.rb:

❮ ALERT: an event that always happens

"Success!" Bill exclaims. "If we schedule this program to run every few minutes, we have a functional first version of RedFlag. Let's show it to the boss."

Sharing Among Events

Your boss is amused by the simplicity of the RedFlag DSL, but she's not completely convinced. "The people who write the events will want to share data among events," she observes. "Can I do this with your DSL? For example, can two separate events access the same variable?" she asks the two of you.

"Of course they can," Bill replies. "We have a *Flat Scope (83)*." To prove that, he whips up a new events file:

blocks/redflag_2/events.rb

```ruby
def monthly_sales
  110   # TODO: read the real number from the database
end

target_sales = 100

event "monthly sales are suspiciously high" do
  monthly_sales > target_sales
end

event "monthly sales are abysmally low" do
  monthly_sales < target_sales
end
```

The two events in this file share a method and a local variable. You run red-flag.rb, and it prints what you expected:

```
ALERT: monthly sales are suspiciously high
```

"Okay, this works," the boss concedes. "But I don't like the idea of variables and methods like monthly_sales and target_sales cluttering the top-level scope. Let me show you what I'd like the DSL to look like instead," she says. Without further ado, the boss grabs the keyboard and starts churning out code like nobody's business.

Quiz: A Better DSL

Where you're left alone to develop a new version of the RedFlag DSL.

Your boss wants you to add a setup instruction to the RedFlag DSL:

blocks/redflag_3/events.rb

```ruby
setup do
  puts "Setting up sky"
  @sky_height = 100
end

setup do
  puts "Setting up mountains"
  @mountains_height = 200
end

event "the sky is falling" do
  @sky_height < 300
end

event "it's getting closer" do
  @sky_height < @mountains_height
end

event "whoops... too late" do
  @sky_height < 0
```

end

In this new version of the DSL, you're free to mix events and setup blocks (*setups* for short). The DSL still checks events, and it also executes all the setups before each event. If you run redflag.rb on the previous test file, you expect this output:

```
Setting up sky
Setting up mountains
ALERT: the sky is falling
Setting up sky
Setting up mountains
ALERT: it's getting closer
Setting up sky
Setting up mountains
```

RedFlag executes all the setups before each of the three events. The first two events generate an alert; the third doesn't.

A setup can set variables by using variable names that begin with an @ sign, such as @sky_height and @mountains_height. Events can then read these variables. Your boss thinks that this feature will encourage programmers to write clean code: all shared variables are initialized together in a setup and then used in events, so it's easy to keep track of variables.

Still impressed by your boss' technical prowess, you and Bill get down to business.

Runaway Bill

You and Bill compare the current RedFlag DSL to the new version your boss has suggested. The current RedFlag executes blocks immediately. The new RedFlag should execute the setups and the events in a specific order. You start by rewriting the event method:

```
def event(description, &block)
  @events << {:description => description, :condition => block}
end

@events = []
load 'events.rb'
```

The new event method converts the event condition from a block to a Proc. Then it wraps the event's description and the Proc-ified condition in a hash and stores the hash in an array of events. The array is a top-level instance variable (like the ones you read about in *Global Variables and Top-Level Instance Variables*, on page 80), so it can be initialized outside the event method. Finally, the last line loads the file that defines the events. Your plan is to write a setup method similar to the event method, and then write the code that executes events and setups in the correct sequence.

As you ponder your next step, Bill slaps his forehead, mutters something about his wife's birthday party, and runs out the door. Now it's up to you alone. Can you complete the new RedFlag DSL and get the expected output from the test file?

Quiz Solution

You can find many different solutions to this quiz. Here is one:

blocks/redflag_3/redflag.rb

```
def setup(&block)
  @setups << block
end

def event(description, &block)
  @events << {:description => description, :condition => block}
end

@setups = []
@events = []
load 'events.rb'

@events.each do |event|
  @setups.each do |setup|
    setup.call
  end
  puts "ALERT: #{event[:description]}" if event[:condition].call
end
```

Both setup and event convert the block to a proc and store away the proc, in @setups and @events, respectively. These two top-level instance variables are shared by setup, event, and the main code.

The main code initializes @setups and @events, then it loads events.rb. The code in the events file calls back into setup and event, adding elements to @setups and @events.

With all the events and setups loaded, your program iterates through the events. For each event, it calls all the setup blocks, and then it calls the event.

You can almost hear the voice of Bill in your head, sounding a bit like Obi-Wan Kenobi: "Those top-level instance variables, @events and @setups, are like global variables in disguise. Why don't you get rid of them?"

Removing the "Global" Variables

To get rid of the global variables (and Bill's voice in your head), you can use a *Shared Scope (84)*:

blocks/redflag_4/redflag.rb

```
lambda {
  setups = []
  events = []

  Kernel.send :define_method, :setup do |&block|
    setups << block
  end

  Kernel.send :define_method, :event do |description, &block|
    events << {:description => description, :condition => block}
  end

  Kernel.send :define_method, :each_setup do |&block|
    setups.each do |setup|
      block.call setup
    end
  end

  Kernel.send :define_method, :each_event do |&block|
    events.each do |event|
      block.call event
    end
  end
}.call

load 'events.rb'

each_event do |event|
  each_setup do |setup|
    setup.call
  end
  puts "ALERT: #{event[:description]}" if event[:condition].call
end
```

The Shared Scope is contained in a lambda that is called immediately. The code in the lambda defines the RedFlag methods as *Kernel Methods (32)* that share two variables: setups and events. Nobody else can see these two variables, because they're local to the lambda. (Indeed, the only reason why we have a lambda here is that we want to make these variables invisible to anyone except the four Kernel Methods.) And yes, each call to Kernel.send is passing a block as an argument to another block.

Now those ugly global variables are gone, but the RedFlag code is not as pleasantly simple as it used to be. It's up to you to decide whether this change is an improvement or just an unwelcome obfuscation. While you decide that, there is one last change that is worth considering.

Adding a Clean Room

In the current version of RedFlag, events can change each other's shared top-level instance variables:

```
event "define a shared variable" do
  @x = 1
end
event "change the variable" do
  @x = @x + 1
end
```

You want events to share variables with setups, but you don't necessarily want events to share variables with each other. Once again, it's up to you to decide whether this is a feature or a potential bug. If you decide that events should be as independent from each other as possible (like tests in a test suite), then you might want to execute events in a *Clean Room (87)*:

blocks/redflag_5/redflag.rb

```
each_event do |event|
  env = Object.new
  each_setup do |setup|
    env.instance_eval &setup
  end
  puts "ALERT: #{event[:description]}" if env.instance_eval &(event[:condition])
end
```

Now an event and its setups are evaluated in the context of an Object that acts as a Clean Room. The instance variables in the setups and events are instance variables of the Clean Room rather than top-level instance variables. Because each event runs in its own Clean Room, events cannot share instance variables.

You might think of using a BasicObject instead of an Object for your Clean Room. However, remember that BasicObject is also a *Blank Slate (66)*, and as such it lacks some common methods, such as puts. So you should only use a BasicObject if you know that the code in the RedFlag events isn't going to call puts or other Object methods. You grin and add a comment to the code, leaving this difficult decision to Bill.

Wrap-Up

Here are a few spells and other interesting things that you learned today:

- What *Scope Gates (81)* are and how Ruby manages scope in general

- How to make bindings visible through scopes with *Flat Scopes (83)* and *Shared Scopes (84)*

- How to execute code in an object's scope (usually with instance_eval or instance_exec), or even in a *Clean Room (87)*

- How to turn a block into an object (a Proc) and back

- How to turn a method into an object (a Method or an UnboundMethod) and back

- What the differences are between the different types of callable objects: blocks, Procs, lambdas, and plain old methods

- How to write your own little DSL

That was a lot of new stuff in a single day. As you sneak out of the office, however, you can't shake the nagging feeling that you'll learn some of Ruby's best-kept secrets tomorrow.

Thursday: Class Definitions

As you know, writing object-oriented programs means spending a good chunk of your time defining classes. In Java and C#, defining a class is like making a deal between you and the compiler. You say, "Here's how my objects are supposed to behave," and the compiler replies, "Okay, they will." Nothing really happens until you create an object of that class and then call that object's methods.

In Ruby, class definitions are different. When you use the class keyword, you aren't just dictating how objects will behave in the future. On the contrary, you're actually *running code.*

If you buy into this notion—that a Ruby class definition is actually regular code that runs—you'll be able to cast some powerful spells. Two such spells that you'll learn about in this chapter are *Class Macros (117)* (methods that modify classes) and *Around Aliases (134)* (methods that wrap additional code around other methods). To help you make the most of these spells, this chapter also describes *singleton classes*, one of Ruby's most elegant features. Singleton classes are an advanced topic, so understanding them will win you bragging rights among Ruby experts.

This chapter also comes with a couple of public service announcements. First, keep in mind that a class is just a souped-up module, so anything you learn about classes also applies to modules. Although I won't repeat this PSA in every section of this chapter, remember that whenever you read about a "class definition," you can also think to yourself "module definition." Second, be prepared: this is probably the most advanced chapter in the entire book. Read through it, and you will be able to walk the darkest corners of the Ruby object model.

Class Definitions Demystified

Where you and Bill tread familiar ground: the Bookworm application and the Ruby object model.

You stumble sleepily into the office, craving your Thursday morning coffee, only to be ambushed by an excited Bill. "Hey!" he says. "Everyone likes the refactorings of Bookworm we did Monday, and the boss wants more. But before we start, let's go over some theory about class definitions. We'll begin where we left off Monday: in the Ruby object model."

Inside Class Definitions

You probably think of a class definition as the place where you define methods. In fact, you can put any code you want in a class definition:

```ruby
class MyClass
  puts 'Hello'
end
```

❮ Hello

Class definitions also return the value of the last statement, just like methods and blocks do:

```ruby
result = class MyClass
  self
end
```

result # => MyClass

This last example emphasizes a compelling point that you might remember from *The self Keyword*, on page 34: in a class (or module) definition, the class itself takes the role of the current object self. Classes and modules are just objects, so why couldn't a class be self? Keep this point about class definitions and self in mind, because the concept will become useful a bit later.

While we're on the topic of self, you can learn about a related concept: that of the current class.

The Current Class

As you know, wherever you are in a Ruby program, you always have a current object: self. Likewise, you always have a *current class* (or module). When you define a method, that method becomes an instance method of the current class.

Although you can get a reference to the current object through self, there's no equivalent keyword to get a reference to the current class. However, in most situations it's easy to keep track of the current class just by looking at the code. Here's how:

- At the top level of your program, the current class is Object, the class of main. (That's why, if you define a method at the top level, that method becomes an instance method of Object.)

- In a method, the current class is the class where the method is defined. Try the following code:

```
class C
  def m1
    def m2; end
  end
end

class D < C; end

obj = D.new
obj.m1

C.instance_methods(false) # => [:m1, :m2]
```

This information is probably going to win you some Ruby trivia contest.

- When you open a class with the class keyword (or a module with the module keyword), that class becomes the current class.

This last case is probably the only one that you care about in practice. Indeed, you use it all the time when you open a class with the class keyword, and define methods in the class with def. However, the class keyword has a limitation: it needs the name of a class. Unfortunately, in some situations you may not know the name of the class that you want to open. For example, think of a method that takes a class and adds a new instance method to it:

```
def add_method_to(a_class)
  # TODO: define method m() on a_class
end
```

How can you open the class if you don't know its name? You need some way other than the class keyword to change the current class. Enter the class_eval method.

class_eval()

Module#class_eval (also known by its alternate name, module_eval) evaluates a block in the context of an existing class:

class_definitions/class_eval.rb

```
def add_method_to(a_class)
  a_class.class_eval do
    def m; 'Hello!'; end
  end
end

add_method_to String
"abc".m    # => "Hello!"
```

Module#class_eval is very different from BasicObject#instance_eval, which you learned about earlier in *instance_eval()*, on page 84. instance_eval only changes self, while class_eval changes both self and the current class.

(This is not the whole truth: instance_eval also changes the current class, but you'll have to wait for *Singleton Classes and instance_eval()*, on page 127, to learn how exactly. For now, you can safely ignore the problem and assume that instance_eval only changes self.)

By changing the current class, class_eval effectively reopens the class, just like the class keyword does.

Module#class_eval is actually more flexible than class. You can use class_eval on any variable that references the class, while class requires a constant. Also, class opens a new scope, losing sight of the current bindings, while class_eval has a *Flat Scope (83)*. As you learned in *Scope Gates*, on page 81, this means you can reference variables from the outer scope in a class_eval block.

Finally, just like instance_eval has a twin method called instance_exec, module_eval/class_eval also has an equivalent module_exec/class_exec method that can pass extra parameters to the block.

Now that you know about both instance_eval and class_eval, you might wonder which of the two you should use. In most cases the answer is easy: you use instance_eval to open an object that is not a class, and class_eval to open a class definition and define methods with def. But what if you want to open an object that happens to be a class (or module) to do something other than using def? Should you use instance_eval or class_eval then?

If all you want is to change self, then both instance_eval and class_eval will do the job nicely. However, you should pick the method that best communicates your intentions. If you're thinking, "I want to open this object, and I don't particularly care that it's a class," then instance_eval is fine. If you're thinking, "I want an *Open Class (14)* here," then class_eval is almost certainly a better match.

That was a lot of information about the current class and how to deal with it. Let's recap the important points that we just went through.

Current Class Wrap-up

You learned a few things about class definitions:

- The Ruby interpreter always keeps a reference to the *current class* (or module). All methods defined with def become instance methods of the current class.

- In a class definition, the current object self and the current class are the same—the class being defined.

- If you have a reference to the class, you can open the class with class_eval (or module_eval).

How can this stuff ever be useful in real life? To show you how you can apply this theory about the current class, let's look at a trick called *Class Instance Variables*.

Class Instance Variables

The Ruby interpreter assumes that all instance variables belong to the current object self. This is also true in a class definition:

class_definitions/class_instance_variables.rb

```
class MyClass
  @my_var = 1
end
```

In a class definition, the role of self belongs to the class itself, so the instance variable @my_var belongs to the class. Don't get confused. Instance variables of the class are different from instance variables of that class's objects, as you can see in the following example:

```
class MyClass
  @my_var = 1
  def self.read; @my_var; end
  def write; @my_var = 2; end
  def read; @my_var; end
end

obj = MyClass.new
obj.read            # => nil
obj.write
obj.read            # => 2
MyClass.read        # => 1
```

The previous code defines two instance variables. Both happen to be named @my_var, but they're defined in different scopes, and they belong to different objects. To see how this works, you have to remember that classes are just objects, and you have to track self through the program. One @my_var is defined with obj as self, so it's an instance variable of the obj object. The other @my_var is defined with MyClass as self, so it's an instance variable of the MyClass object —a *Class Instance Variable.*

Spell: Class Instance Variable, page 232

If you come from Java, you may be tempted to think that Class Instance Variables are similar to Java's "static fields." Instead, they're just regular instance variables that happen to belong to an object of class Class. Because of that, a Class Instance Variable can be accessed only by the class itself— not by an instance or by a subclass.

We've touched on many things: the current class, class definitions, self, class_eval, Class Instance Variables…. Now you can go back to Bookworm and put these features together.

Working on Bookworm Again

The Bookworm source contains very few unit tests, so it's up to you and Bill to write tests as you refactor. Sometimes this proves to be difficult, as is the case with this class:

`class_definitions/bookworm_classvars.rb`

```
class Loan
  def initialize(book)
    @book = book
    @time = Time.now
  end

  def to_s
    "#{@book.upcase} loaned on #{@time}"
  end
end
```

Loan stores the title of a book and the time when it was loaned—that is, the time when the object was created. You'd like to write a unit test for the to_s method, but to write that test, you'd have to know the exact time when the object was created. This is a common problem with code that relies on Time or Date: such code returns a different result every time it runs, so you don't know what result to test for.

"I think I have a solution to this problem," Bill announces. "It's a bit involved, so it will require some attention on your part. Here it is."

Class Variables

If you want to store a variable in a class, you have more options than just using a *Class Instance Variable (110)*. You can also use a *class variable*, identified by an @@ prefix:

```
class C
  @@v = 1
end
```

Class variables are different from Class Instance Variables because they can be accessed by subclasses and by regular instance methods. (In that respect, they're more similar to Java's static fields.)

```
class D < C
  def my_method; @@v; end
end

D.new.my_method  # => 1
```

Unfortunately, class variables have a nasty habit of surprising you. Here's an example:

```
@@v = 1

class MyClass
  @@v = 2
end

@@v  # => 2
```

You get this result because class variables don't really belong to classes—they belong to class *hierarchies*. Because @@v is defined in the context of main, it belongs to main's class Object…and to all the descendants of Object. MyClass inherits from Object, so it ends up sharing the same class variable. As technically sound as this behavior is, it's still likely to trip you.

Because of unwelcome surprises like the one shown earlier, most Rubyists nowadays shun class variables in favor of Class Instance Variables. Also, Ruby 2.x issues a stern warning whenever you access a class variable from the top level.

```
class Loan
  def initialize(book)
    @book = book
➤   @time = Loan.time_class.now
  end

➤ def self.time_class
➤   @time_class || Time
➤ end

  def to_s
    # ...
```

Loan.time_class returns a class, and Loan#initialize uses that class to get the time. The class is stored in a *Class Instance Variable (110)* named @time_class. If @time_class is nil, the *Nil Guard (219)* in time_class returns the Time class as a default.

In production, Loan always uses the Time class, because @time_class is always nil. By contrast, the unit tests can rely on a fake time class that always returns the same value. The tests can assign a value to the private @time_class variable by using either class_eval or instance_eval. Either of the two methods will do here, because they both change self:

```ruby
class FakeTime
  def self.now; 'Mon Apr 06 12:15:50'; end
end

require 'test/unit'

class TestLoan < Test::Unit::TestCase
  def test_conversion_to_string
    Loan.instance_eval { @time_class = FakeTime }
    loan = Loan.new('War and Peace')
    assert_equal 'WAR AND PEACE loaned on Mon Apr 06 12:15:50', loan.to_s
  end
end
```

Bill is quite proud of his own coding prowess. He says, "I think we deserve a break—after I give you a quiz."

Quiz: Class Taboo

Where you write an entire program without ever using a certain popular keyword.

Did you ever play *Taboo*?[1] The rules are simple: you're given a secret word and a list of words that you cannot use. (They are "taboo.") You must help a teammate guess the secret word. You can give your teammate as many suggestions as you want, but you must never say a taboo word. If you do that, you lose immediately.

Your challenge: play *Taboo* with Ruby code. You have only one taboo word, the class keyword. Your "secret word" is actually a Ruby class:

```ruby
class MyClass < Array
  def my_method
    'Hello!'
  end
end
```

---

1. http://en.wikipedia.org/wiki/Taboo_(game).

You have to write a piece of code that has exactly the same effect as the previous one, without ever using the class keyword. Are you up to the challenge? (Just one hint: look at the documentation for Class.new.)

Quiz Solution

Because a class is just an instance of Class, you can create it by calling Class.new. Class.new also accepts an argument (the superclass of the new class) and a block that is evaluated in the context of the newborn class:

```
c = Class.new(Array) do
  def my_method
    'Hello!'
  end
end
```

Now you have a variable that references a class, but the class is still anonymous. Do you remember the discussion about class names in *Constants*, on page 21? The name of a class is just a constant, so you can assign it yourself:

```
MyClass = c
```

Interestingly, Ruby is cheating a little here. When you assign an anonymous class to a constant, Ruby understands that you're trying to give a name to the class, and it does something special: it turns around to the class and says, "Here's your new name." Now the constant references the Class, and the Class also references the constant. If it weren't for this trick, a class wouldn't be able to know its own name, and you couldn't write this:

```
c.name     # => "MyClass"
```

You turn to Bill to show him your solution to the quiz—but he's already busy browsing the Bookworm source. It's time to get back to the task at hand.

Singleton Methods

Where it's your turn to teach Bill a few tricks.

It's late morning, and you and Bill are deep in the flow. You're zipping through the Bookworm source, deleting a useless line here, changing a confusing name there, and generally polishing the code...until you bump into a particularly troublesome bit of refactoring.

The Paragraph class wraps a string and then delegates all calls to the wrapped string—all of them, that is, except for one method, Paragraph#title?, which returns true if a Paragraph is all uppercase.

`class_definitions/paragraph.rb`

```ruby
class Paragraph
  def initialize(text)
    @text = text
  end

  def title?; @text.upcase == @text; end
  def reverse; @text.reverse; end
  def upcase; @text.upcase; end
  # ...
```

Paragraph objects are created in a single place in the Bookworm source code. Also, Paragraph#title? is called only once in the whole application, from a method named index:

```ruby
def index(paragraph)
  add_to_index(paragraph) if paragraph.title?
end
```

Bill frowns. "The stupid Paragraph class really doesn't hold its own weight. We could scrap it entirely and just use regular Strings, if it weren't for the title? method."

"Why don't we *Monkeypatch (16)* the String class and add the title? method right there?" you offer. "I'm not convinced," Bill says. "A method with that name would make sense only on strings that represent a paragraph, not on each and every string."

While Bill is pondering the idea of patching the String class with a *Refinement (36)*, you decide to Google for a solution.

Introducing Singleton Methods

As it turns out, Ruby allows you to add a method to a single object. For example, here's how you can add title? to a specific string:

`class_definitions/singleton_methods.rb`

```ruby
str = "just a regular string"

def str.title?
  self.upcase == self
end

str.title?                  # => false
str.methods.grep(/title?/)  # => [:title?]
str.singleton_methods       # => [:title?]
```

The previous code adds a method named title? to str. No other object gets the method—not even other Strings. A method like this one, which is specific to a single object, is called a *Singleton Method*. You can define a Singleton Method with either the syntax above or the `Object#define_singleton_method` method.

Spell: Singleton Method, page 242

Thanks to Singleton Methods, you can now fix your problem with the Book-worm source. You can send any old `String` to `index` if you enhance that `String` with a `title?` Singleton Method:

`class_definitions/paragraph.rb`

```
paragraph = "any string can be a paragraph"

def paragraph.title?
  self.upcase == self
end

index(paragraph)
```

Now you can use plain strings in Bookworm and delete the `Paragraph` class.

Bill is awestruck by your solution. "I knew about Singleton Methods, but I never realized you could use them this way."

"Wait a minute," you reply. "You *knew* about them? What did you think they were useful for?"

"Singleton Methods aren't just useful for enhancing a specific object, like you just did." Bill replies. "They're also the basis for one of Ruby's most common features. What if I told you that you've been using Singleton Methods all along, without ever knowing it?"

The Truth About Class Methods

Remember what you learned in *Inside the Object Model*, on page 16? Classes are just objects, and class names are just constants. If you remember this concept, then you'll see that calling a method on a class is the same as calling a method on an object:

```
an_object.a_method
AClass.a_class_method
```

See? The first line calls a method on an object referenced by a variable, and the second line calls a method on an object (that also happens to be a class) referenced by a constant. It's the same syntax.

But, wait—there's more. Remember how Bill told you that you've been using *Singleton Methods (115)* all along? That's really what class methods are: they're *Singleton Methods of a class*. In fact, if you compare the definition of a Single-ton Method and the definition of a class method, you'll see that they're the same:

Duck Typing

Some people are horrified by *Singleton Methods (115)*, thinking that if each object can have its own methods, no matter which class it belongs to, then your code is going to become a twisted tangle of spaghetti.

If you reacted that way yourself, then you're probably used to static languages. In a static language such as Java, you say that an object has type T because it belongs to class T (or because it implements interface T). In a dynamic language such as Ruby, the "type" of an object is not strictly related to its class. Instead, the "type" is simply the set of methods to which an object can respond.

People refer to this second, more fluid notion of a type as *duck typing*, referring to the saying: "if it walks like a duck and quacks like a duck, then it must be a duck." In other words, you don't care that an object is an instance of class Duck. You just care that it responds to walk and quack, whether they're regular methods, *Singleton Methods (115)*, or even *Ghost Methods (57)*.

If you hang around Ruby for a while, you will get used to duck typing—and after learning a few cool dynamic tricks, you might even wonder how you could have lived without it in the first place.

```
def obj.a_singleton_method; end
def MyClass.another_class_method; end
```

So, the syntax for defining a Singleton Method with def is always the same:

```
def object.method
  # Method body here
end
```

In the definition shown previously, object can be an object reference, a constant class name, or self. The syntax might look different in the three cases, but in truth the underlying mechanism is always the same. Nice design, don't you think?

You're not quite finished with class methods yet. There's a very useful and common spell that relies on class methods exclusively, and it deserves its own discussion.

Class Macros

Look at this example, coming straight from the core of Ruby.

The attr_accessor() Example

Ruby objects don't have attributes. If you want something that looks like an attribute, you have to define two *Mimic Methods (218)*, a reader and a writer:

```
class_definitions/attr.rb
```

```ruby
class MyClass
  def my_attribute=(value)
    @my_attribute = value
  end

  def my_attribute
    @my_attribute
  end
end
obj = MyClass.new
obj.my_attribute = 'x'
obj.my_attribute          # => "x"
```

Writing methods like these (also called *accessors*) gets boring quickly. As an alternative, you can generate accessors by using one of the methods in the Module#attr_* family. Module#attr_reader generates the reader, Module#attr_writer generates the writer, and Module#attr_accessor generates both:

```ruby
class MyClass
  attr_accessor :my_attribute
end
```

All the attr_* methods are defined on class Module, so you can use them whenever self is a module or a class. A method such as attr_accessor is called a *Class Macro*. Class Macros look like keywords, but they're just regular class methods that are meant to be used in a class definition.

Spell: Class Macro, page 233

"Now that you know about Class Macros," Bill says, "I think I know a place in Bookworm's source code where we can make good use of them."

Class Macros Applied

The Book class in the Bookworm source code has methods named GetTitle, title2, and LEND_TO_USER. By Ruby's conventions, these methods should be named title, subtitle, and lend_to, respectively. However, there are other projects that use the Book class, and you have no control over these projects. If you just rename the methods, you will break the callers.

Bill has an idea to fix this situation: you can rename the methods if you invent a *Class Macro (117)* that deprecates the old names:

```
class_definitions/deprecated.rb
```

```ruby
class Book
  def title # ...

  def subtitle # ...

  def lend_to(user)
```

```
    puts "Lending to #{user}"
    # ...
  end

  def self.deprecate(old_method, new_method)
    define_method(old_method) do |*args, &block|
      warn "Warning: #{old_method}() is deprecated. Use #{new_method}()."
      send(new_method, *args, &block)
    end
  end

  deprecate :GetTitle, :title
  deprecate :LEND_TO_USER, :lend_to
  deprecate :title2, :subtitle
end
```

The deprecate method takes the old name and the new name of a method and
defines a *Dynamic Method (51)* that catches calls to the old name. The
Dynamic Method forwards the calls to the renamed method—but first it prints
a warning on the console to notify the callers that the old name has been
deprecated:

```
b = Book.new
b.LEND_TO_USER("Bill")
```

```
Warning: LEND_TO_USER() is deprecated. Use lend_to().
Lending to Bill
```

That was an ingenious way to use a Class Macro. However, if you really want
to understand Class Macros, as well as Singleton Methods in general, you
have to fit one last missing piece in the Ruby object model.

Singleton Classes

Where you place the final piece in the object model puzzle.

Singleton classes are the UFOs of the Ruby world: even if you never see one
in person, you can find scattered hints of their existence all over the place.
Let's start our investigation into this difficult subject by collecting some evidence. (Be aware that the next few pages contain advanced material that
might take a while for you to digest. If you want, you can skip straight to
Method Wrappers, on page 131, on your first read through and come back to
this section later.)

The Mystery of Singleton Methods

In *Method Lookup*, on page 28, you learned how Ruby finds methods by going
right into the receiver's class and then *up* the class hierarchy. For example:

```
class MyClass
  def my_method; end
end

obj = MyClass.new
obj.my_method
```

Bill draws a flowchart and says, "When you call my_method, Ruby goes right into MyClass and finds the method there." So far, so good.

Now, what happens if you define a *Singleton Method (115)* on obj?

```
def obj.my_singleton_method; end
```

If you look at the previous flowchart, you'll notice that there's no obvious home for my_singleton_method there.

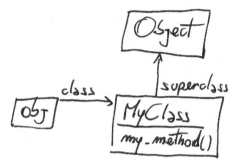

The Singleton Method can't live in obj, because obj is not a class. It can't live in MyClass, because if it did, all instances of MyClass would share it. And it cannot be an instance method of MyClass's superclass, Object. So then, where do Singleton Methods live?

Class methods are a special kind of Singleton Method—and just as baffling:

```
def MyClass.my_class_method; end
```

If you look at the following figure, you'll find that, again, my_class_method doesn't seem to live anywhere in Bill's diagram.

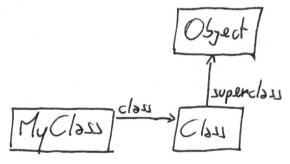

The explanation of this mystery could surprise you.

Singleton Classes Revealed

When you ask an object for its class, Ruby doesn't always tell you the whole truth. Instead of the class that you see, an object can have its own special, hidden class. That's called the *singleton class* of the object. (You can also hear it called the *metaclass* or the *eigenclass*. However, "singleton class" is the official name.)

Methods like `Object#class` keep the singleton class carefully hidden, but you can work around them. Ruby has a special syntax, based on the class keyword, that places you in the scope of the singleton class:

```
class << an_object
  # your code here
end
```

If you want to get a reference to the singleton class, you can return self out of the scope:

```
obj = Object.new

singleton_class = class << obj
  self
end

singleton_class.class   # => Class
```

That sneaky singleton class was trying to hide, but we managed to find it.

Back in Ruby's old days, you had to return self like we just did to get a reference to the singleton class. These days you can also get a reference to the singleton class with the handy `Object#singleton_class` method:

```
"abc".singleton_class     # => #<Class:#<String:0x331df0>>
```

The previous example also shows that a singleton class is a class—but a very special one. For starters, it's invisible until you resort to either `Object#singleton_class`, or the exotic `class <<` syntax. Also, singleton classes have only a single instance (that's where their name comes from), and they can't be inherited. More important, *a singleton class is where an object's Singleton Methods live*:

```
def obj.my_singleton_method; end
singleton_class.instance_methods.grep(/my_/)   # => [:my_singleton_method]
```

To fully understand the consequences of this last point, you have to look deeper into Ruby's object model.

Method Lookup Revisited

In *What Happens When You Call a Method?*, on page 27, you learned about the Ruby object model and method lookup. Back then, we had to leave some parts of the object model unexplored. Singleton classes are the missing link we needed. Once you understand singleton classes, all the bits and pieces in the object model finally fall into place.

Method Lookup Review

To look into the object model, you need a practical example to focus on. Let's write a "lab rat" program:

```
class C
  def a_method
    'C#a_method()'
  end
end

class D < C; end

obj = D.new
obj.a_method     # => "C#a_method()"
```

If you draw a picture of obj and its ancestors chain, it will probably look like the following figure. (For now, you don't have to bother with singleton classes or modules.)

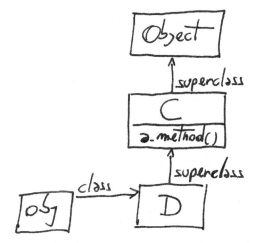

You know that method lookup goes one step to the right, then up. When you call obj.a_method(), Ruby goes *right* into obj's class D. From there, it climbs *up* the ancestors chain until it finds a_method in class C. Now, let's add singleton classes to the mix.

Singleton Classes and Method Lookup

As you explore singleton classes, you may notice that their names are not meant to be uttered by humans. When you print it on the screen, a singleton class looks something like this:

```
obj = Object.new
obj.singleton_class   # => #<Class:#<Object:0x007fd96909b588>>
```

The diagrams in the rest of this chapter identify singleton classes with a simple # prefix. By this convention, #obj is the singleton class of obj, #C is the singleton class of C, and so on.

Armed with the singleton_class method and your new naming convention, you can now proceed with your fearless exploration of the object model. Let's go back to the "lab rat" program and define a *Singleton Method (115)*.

```
class << obj
  def a_singleton_method
    'obj#a_singleton_method()'
  end
end
```

Now for an experiment. You know that a singleton class is a class, so it must have a superclass. Which is the superclass of the singleton class?

```
obj.singleton_class.superclass   # => D
```

The superclass of obj's singleton class is D. Try adding this newfound knowledge to the diagram of the "lab rat" object model. The result is shown in Figure 6, *Method lookup with singleton classes*, on page 123.

You can see how Singleton Methods fit into the normal process of method lookup. If an object has a singleton class, Ruby starts looking for methods in the singleton class rather than the conventional class, and that's why you can call Singleton Methods such as obj#a_singleton_method. If Ruby can't find the method in the singleton class, then it goes up the ancestors chain, ending in the superclass of the singleton class—which is the object's class. From there, everything is business as usual.

Now you understand how Singleton Methods work. But what about class methods? Yes, they're just a special case of Singleton Methods, but they deserve a closer look.

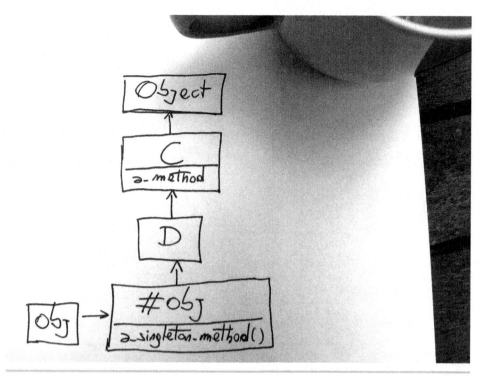

Figure 6—Method lookup with singleton classes

Singleton Classes and Inheritance

In this section, we're going to look at the connections between classes, singleton classes, and superclasses. This area of the object model can be a real brain-twister. Once it clicks in your mind, however, it will feel elegant and beautiful. If you're stuck, just look at the pictures or fire up irb and experiment on your own.

Try adding a class method to the "lab rat" program.

```ruby
class C
  class << self
    def a_class_method
      'C.a_class_method()'
    end
  end
end
```

Now you can explore the resulting object model. (As you do that, keep in mind that singleton classes became slightly more visible in Ruby 2.1. Starting from that version, if you ask a singleton class for its ancestors, the result will include ancestors that are themselves singleton classes. Until Ruby 2.0, ancestors always shows regular classes only.)

```
C.singleton_class               # => #<Class:C>
D.singleton_class               # => #<Class:D>
D.singleton_class.superclass    # => #<Class:C>
C.singleton_class.superclass    # => #<Class:Object>
```

Bill grabs a scrap of paper and draws the following diagram.

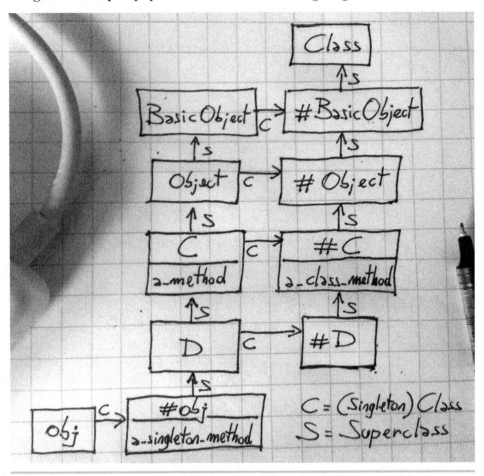

Figure 7—Singleton classes and inheritance

This is a somewhat complicated diagram. The arrows marked with S link classes to their superclasses, and the arrows marked with C link objects (including classes) to their classes, which in this case are all singleton classes. The arrows marked with a C do *not* point at the same classes that the class method would return, because the class method doesn't know about singleton classes. For example, obj.class would return D, even if the class of obj is actually its singleton class, #obj.

This diagram doesn't include modules. If you're a completist, you can draw the Kernel module between Object and BasicObject. On the other hand, you probably don't want to include #Kernel in this diagram. Although modules can have singleton classes like any other object, the singleton class of Kernel is not part of obj's or #D's ancestor chains.

Apparently, Ruby organizes classes, singleton classes, and superclasses in a very purposeful pattern. The superclass of #D is #C, which is also the singleton class of C. By the same rule, the superclass of #C is #Object. Bill tries to sum it all up, making things even more confusing: "The superclass of the singleton class is the singleton class of the superclass. It's easy."

This complicated arrangement of classes, superclasses, and singleton classes can be baffling. Why does Ruby go to such lengths to organize the object model this way? The reason is that thanks to this arrangement, you can call a class method on a subclass:

```
D.a_class_method          # => "C.a_class_method()"
```

Even if a_class_method is defined on C, you can also call it on D. This is probably what you expect, but it's only possible because method lookup starts in #D and goes up to #D's superclass #C, where it finds the method.

Ingenious, isn't it? Now you can finally grasp the entire object model.

The Great Unified Theory

"The Ruby object model is a beautiful place," Bill notes, with a dreamy expression on his face. "There are classes, singleton classes, and modules. There are instance methods, class methods, and Singleton Methods."

At first glance, it all looks very complex. Look closer, and the complexity fades away. If you put singleton classes together with regular classes and modules, you end up with the seven rules of the Ruby object model:

1. There is only one kind of object—be it a regular object or a module.

2. There is only one kind of module—be it a regular module, a class, or a singleton class.

3. There is only one kind of method, and it lives in a module—most often in a class.

Meta Squared

Singleton classes are classes, and classes are objects, and objects have singleton classes.... Can you see where this train of thought is going? Like any other object, a singleton class must have its own singleton class:

```
class << "abc"
  class << self
    self  # => #<Class:#<Class:#<String:0x33552c>>>
  end
end
```

If you ever find a practical use for singleton classes of singleton classes, let the world know.

4. Every object, classes included, has its own "real class," be it a regular class or a singleton class.

5. Every class, with the exception of BasicObject, has exactly one ancestor—either a superclass or a module. This means you have a single chain of ancestors from any class up to BasicObject.

6. The superclass of the singleton class of an object is the object's class. The superclass of the singleton class of a class is the singleton class of the class's superclass. (Try repeating that three times, fast. Then look back at Figure 7, *Singleton classes and inheritance*, on page 124, and it will all make sense.)

7. When you call a method, Ruby goes "right" in the receiver's real class and then "up" the ancestors chain. That's all there is to know about the way Ruby finds methods.

Any Ruby programmer can stumble on a difficult question about the object model. "Which method in this complicated hierarchy gets called first?" Or maybe, "Can I call this method from that object?" When this happens to you, review the seven rules listed earlier, maybe draw a quick diagram of the object model, and you'll find the answer in no time at all.

Congratulations—you now understand the entire Ruby object model.

Class Methods Syntaxes

Because class methods are just Singleton Methods that live in the class's singleton class, now you have three different ways to define a class method. They're shown in the following code.

```ruby
def MyClass.a_class_method; end

class MyClass
  def self.another_class_method; end
end

class MyClass
  class << self
    def yet_another_class_method; end
  end
end
```

The first syntax is usually frowned upon by expert Rubyists because it duplicates the class name, making it more difficult to refactor. The second syntax takes advantage of the fact that self in the class definition is the class itself. The third syntax is the trickiest one: the code opens the singleton class and defines the method in there. This last syntax acknowledges the singleton class explicitly, so it will win you some street cred in Ruby circles.

Singleton Classes and instance_eval()

Now that you know about singleton classes, you can also fill in one missing snippet of knowledge about the instance_eval method. In *class_eval()*, on page 107, you learned that instance_eval changes self, and class_eval changes both self and the current class. However, instance_eval also changes the current class; it changes it to the *singleton class* of the receiver. This example uses instance_eval to define a *Singleton Method (115)*:

`class_definitions/instance_eval.rb`

```ruby
s1, s2 = "abc", "def"

s1.instance_eval do
  def swoosh!; reverse; end
end

s1.swoosh!                # => "cba"
s2.respond_to?(:swoosh!)  # => false
```

You'll rarely, if ever, see instance_eval used purposefully to change the current class, as in the example above. The standard meaning of instance_eval is this: "I want to change self."

Class Attributes

Bill's detailed explanations have left you a bit perplexed. "Okay," you say, "I can see how singleton classes are useful to understanding the object model. But how do I use them in practice?"

Let's look at an example involving *Class Macros (117)*. Do you remember the attr_accessor method from *The attr_accessor() Example*, on page 116? It generates attributes for any object:

class_definitions/class_attr.rb

```ruby
class MyClass
  attr_accessor :a
end

obj = MyClass.new
obj.a = 2
obj.a           # => 2
```

But what if you want to define an attribute on a *class* instead? You might be tempted to reopen Class and define the attribute there:

```ruby
class MyClass; end

class Class
  attr_accessor :b
end

MyClass.b = 42
MyClass.b        # => 42
```

This works, but it adds the attribute to *all* classes. If you want an attribute that's specific to MyClass, you need a different technique. Define the attribute in the singleton class:

```ruby
class MyClass
  class << self
    attr_accessor :c
  end
end

MyClass.c = 'It works!'
MyClass.c                # => "It works!"
```

To understand how this works, remember that an attribute is actually a pair of methods. If you define those methods in the singleton class, they become class methods, as if you'd written this:

```ruby
def MyClass.c=(value)
  @c = value
end

def MyClass.c
  @c
end
```

As usual, Bill grabs the nearest available scrap of paper and scribbles the following diagram on it. "That's how you define an attribute on a class," he says.

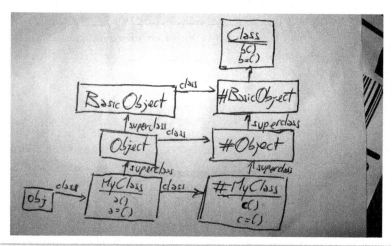

Figure 8—Class attributes live in the class's singleton class.

You can also see another interesting detail in this diagram. The superclass of #BasicObject is none other than good old Class. This fact explains why you can call MyClass.b and MyClass.b=.

Clearly happy with his own explanation, Bill leans back in his comfy chair. "Cool stuff, huh? Now, let's try a little quiz."

Quiz: Module Trouble

Where you learn that singleton classes and modules mix well with each other.

Bill decides it's time for a story: "Every single day, somewhere in the world, a Ruby programmer tries to define a class method by including a module. I tried it myself, but it didn't work."

class_definitions/module_trouble_failure.rb

```ruby
module MyModule
  def self.my_method; 'hello'; end
end

class MyClass
  include MyModule
end

MyClass.my_method   # NoMethodError!
```

"You see," Bill continues, "when a class includes a module, it gets the module's instance methods—*not* the class methods. Class methods stay out of reach, in the module's singleton class."

"So, how did you find a solution?" you ask. "Oh, I didn't," Bill replies, blushing. "I just asked for the solution on a mailing list, like everybody else does. But maybe *you* can find a solution." Think about the object model and singleton classes. How would you modify the code that you just looked at so that it works as expected?

Quiz Solution

The solution to this quiz is simple and subtle at the same time. First, define my_method as a regular instance method of MyModule. Then include the module in the singleton class of MyClass.

class_definitions/module_trouble_solution.rb

```
module MyModule
➤   def my_method; 'hello'; end
end

class MyClass
➤   class << self
➤     include MyModule
➤   end
end

MyClass.my_method    # => "hello"
```

my_method is an instance method of the singleton class of MyClass. As such, my_method is also a class method of MyClass. This technique is called a *Class Extension*.

Spell: Class Extension, page 232

"That's brilliant," Bill says. "What about trying the same trick on a regular object instead of a class?"

Class Methods and include()

Reviewing Class Extensions, you can define class methods by mixing them into the class's singleton class. Class methods are just a special case of Singleton Methods, so you can generalize this trick to any object. In the general case, this is called an *Object Extension*. In the following example, obj is extended with the instance methods of MyModule:

Spell: Object Extension, page 239

class_definitions/module_trouble_object.rb

```
module MyModule
  def my_method; 'hello'; end
end
```

```
obj = Object.new

class << obj
  include MyModule
end

obj.my_method          # => "hello"
obj.singleton_methods  # => [:my_method]
```

In case you think that opening the singleton class is a clumsy way to extend a class or an object, let's also look at an alternative technique.

Object#extend

Class Extensions (130) and *Object Extensions (130)* are common enough that Ruby provides a method just for them, named Object#extend:

`class_definitions/module_trouble_extend.rb`

```
module MyModule
  def my_method; 'hello'; end
end

obj = Object.new
obj.extend MyModule
obj.my_method         # => "hello"

class MyClass
  extend MyModule
end

MyClass.my_method     # => "hello"
```

Object#extend is simply a shortcut that includes a module in the receiver's singleton class. You can always do that yourself, if you so choose.

"Enough talking about singleton classes today," Bill announces. "I don't want to get a meta-headache. For now, let's go back to refactoring Bookworm."

Method Wrappers

Where you learn how to wrap a method inside another method—three different ways.

As the day draws to a close, you and Bill find yourselves stuck. Many methods in Bookworm rely on an open source library that retrieves a book's reviews from Amazon's website. The following code shows one example:

```
def deserves_a_look?(book)
  amazon = Amazon.new
  amazon.reviews_of(book).size > 20
end
```

This code works in most cases, but it doesn't manage exceptions. If a remote call to Amazon fails, Bookworm itself should log this problem and proceed. You could easily add exception management to each line in Bookworm that calls deserves_a_look?—but there are tens of such lines, and you don't want to change all of them.

To sum up the problem: you have a method that you don't want to modify directly because it's in a library. You want to wrap additional functionality around this method so that all clients get the additional functionality automatically. You can do this in a few ways, but to get to the first of them you need to know about *aliases*.

Around Aliases

You can give an alternate name to a Ruby method by using Module#alias_method:

class_definitions/alias.rb

```
class MyClass
  def my_method; 'my_method()'; end
  alias_method :m, :my_method
end

obj = MyClass.new
obj.my_method   # => "my_method()"
obj.m           # => "my_method()"
```

In alias_method, the new name for the method comes first, and the original name comes second. You can provide the names either as symbols or as strings.

(Ruby also has an alias keyword, which is an alternative to Module#alias_method. It can be useful if you want to alias a method at the top level, where Module#alias_method is not available.)

Continuing with the previous example:

```
class MyClass
  alias_method :m2, :m
end

obj.m2          # => "my_method()"
```

Aliases are common everywhere in Ruby, including the core libraries. For example, String#size is an alias of String#length, and the Integer class has a method with no fewer than five different names. (Can you spot it?)

What happens if you alias a method and then redefine it? You can try this with a simple program:

```
class_definitions/wrapper_around_alias.rb
```

```ruby
class String
  alias_method :real_length, :length

  def length
    real_length > 5 ? 'long' : 'short'
  end
end

"War and Peace".length      # => "long"
"War and Peace".real_length # => 13
```

The previous code redefines String#length, but the alias still refers to the original method. This gives you insight into how method redefinition works. When you redefine a method, you don't really change the method. Instead, you define a new method and attach an existing name to that new method. You can still call the old version of the method as long as you have another name that's still attached to it.

This idea of aliasing a method and then redefining it is the basis of an interesting trick—one that deserves its own example.

The Thor Example

Thor is a Ruby gem for building command-line utilities. Some versions of Thor include a program named rake2thor that converts Rake build files to Thor scripts. As part of doing that, rake2thor must load a Rakefile and store away the names of all the files that are in turn required from that Rakefile. Here is the code where the magic happens:

```
gems/thor-0.17.0/bin/rake2thor
```

```ruby
input   = ARGV[0] || 'Rakefile'
$requires = []

module Kernel
  def require_with_record(file)
    $requires << file if caller[1] =~ /rake2thor:/
    require_without_record file
  end
  alias_method :require_without_record, :require
  alias_method :require, :require_with_record
end

load input
```

The code above prepares a global array to store the names of the required files; then it opens the Kernel module and plays a few tricks with method aliases; and finally, it loads the Rakefile. Focus on the middle part—the code dealing with Kernel. To understand what is going on there, look at this slightly simplified version of the original code:

```ruby
module Kernel
  alias_method :require_without_record, :require

  def require(file)
    $requires << file if caller[1] =~ /rake2thor:/
    require_without_record file
  end
end
```

The *Open Class (14)* above does three things. First, it aliases the standard Kernel#require method to another name (require_without_record). Second, it *Monkey-patches (16)* require to store the names of files that are required by the Rakefile. (It does that by getting the stack of callers with the Kernel#caller method. If the second caller in the stack is rake2thor itself, this means that the Rakefile must be the first caller in the stack—the one that actually called require.) Finally, the new require falls back to the original require, now called require_without_record.

Compared to this simplified version, the original rake2thor code goes one step further: it also creates an alias for the new require called require_with_record. While this latest alias makes the methods more explicit, the important result is pretty much the same in both versions of the code: Kernel#require has changed, and the new require is "wrapped around" the old require. That's why this trick is called an *Around Alias*.

Spell: Around Alias, page 231

You can write an Around Alias in three simple steps:

1. You alias a method.

2. You redefine it.

3. You call the old method from the new method.

One downside of Around Aliases is that they pollute your classes with one additional method name. You can fix this small problem somehow by making the old version of the method private after you alias it. (In Ruby it's the method's name, not the method itself, that is either public or private.)

Another potential problem of Around Aliases has to do with loading. You should never load an Around Alias twice, unless you want to end up with an exception when you call the method. Can you see why?

The main issue with Around Aliases, however, is that they are a form of Monkeypatching. Like all Monkeypatches, they can break existing code that wasn't expecting the method to change. For this reason, Ruby 2.0 introduced not one, but two additional ways to wrap additional functionality around an existing method.

More Method Wrappers

In *Refinements*, on page 36, you learned that a *Refinement (36)* works like a patch of code that has been slapped directly over a class. However, Refinements have one additional feature that enables you to use them in place of *Around Aliases (134)*: if you call super from a refined method, you will call the original, unrefined method. Here comes an example:

class_definitions/wrapper_refinement.rb

```ruby
module StringRefinement
  refine String do
    def length
      super > 5 ? 'long' : 'short'
    end
  end
end

using StringRefinement

"War and Peace".length      # => "long"
```

The code above refines the String class to wrap additional functionality around its length method. Like other Refinements, this *Refinement Wrapper* applies only until the end of the file (or, in Ruby 2.1, the module definition). This makes it generally safer than the equivalent Around Alias, which applies everywhere.

Spell: Refinement Wrapper, page 240

Finally, you have a third way of wrapping a method: you can use Module#prepend, which you might remember from *Modules and Lookup*, on page 30. Module#prepend works a bit like include, but it inserts the module *below* the includer in the chain of ancestors, rather than above it. This means that a method in a prepended module can override a method in the includer and call the non-overridden version with super:

class_definitions/wrapper_prepend.rb

```ruby
module ExplicitString
  def length
    super > 5 ? 'long' : 'short'
  end
end

String.class_eval do
  prepend ExplicitString
end

"War and Peace".length      # => "long"
```

Spell: Prepended Wrapper, page 239

You can call this a *Prepended Wrapper*. It's not local like a Refinement Wrapper, but it's generally considered cleaner and more explicit than both a Refinement Wrapper and an Around Alias.

Now you know more than enough to get back to the Bookworm source code.

Solving the Amazon Problem

Remember where this discussion of method wrappers originated? You and Bill wanted to wrap logging and exception handling around the Amazon#reviews_of method. Now you can finally do that with an *Around Alias (134)*, a *Refinement Wrapper (135)*, or a *Prepended Wrapper (136)*. The third option looks cleaner, as it doesn't dabble in Monkeypatching or weird Refinement rules:

class_definitions/bookworm_wrapper.rb

```
module AmazonWrapper
  def reviews_of(book)
    start = Time.now
    result = super
    time_taken = Time.now - start
    puts "reviews_of() took more than #{time_taken} seconds" if time_taken > 2
    result
  rescue
    puts "reviews_of() failed"
    []
  end
end

Amazon.class_eval do
  prepend AmazonWrapper
end
```

As you admire this smart piece of code, Bill hits you with an unexpected quiz.

Quiz: Broken Math

Where you find that one plus one doesn't always equal two.

Most Ruby operators are actually methods. For example, the + operator on integers is syntactic sugar for a method named Fixnum#+. When you write 1 + 1, the parser internally converts it to 1.+(1).

The cool thing about methods is that you can redefine them. So, here's your challenge: break the rules of math by redefining Fixnum#+ so that it always returns the correct result plus one. For example:

```
1 + 1    # => 3
```

Quiz Solution

You can solve this quiz with an *Open Class (14)*. Just reopen Fixnum and redefine + so that (x + y) becomes (x + y + 1). This is not as easy as it seems, however. The new version of + relies on the old version of +, so you need to wrap your old version with the new version. You can do that with an *Around Alias (134)*:

class_definitions/broken_math.rb

```
class Fixnum
  alias_method :old_plus, :+

  def +(value)
    self.old_plus(value).old_plus(1)
  end
end
```

Now you have the power to wreak havoc on Ruby's basic arithmetic. Enjoy this code responsibly.

Wrap-Up

You covered a lot of ground today. Let's sum it all up:

- You looked at the effects of class definitions on self (the default receiver of the methods you call) and on the current class (the default home of the methods you define).

- You made acquaintance with *Singleton Methods (115)* and singleton classes, gaining new insights into the object model and method lookup.

- You added a few new tricks to your bag, including *Class Instance Variables (110)*, *Class Macros (117)*, and *Prepended Wrappers (136)*.

Also remember that today you used the word "class" as a shortcut to "class or module," and everything you learned about classes can also be applied to modules: the "current class" might actually be a module, a "class instance variable" could well be a "module instance variable," and so on.

That was quite a deep dive into Ruby's object model. As the two of you prepare to leave the office, Bill makes a promise that tomorrow will be less talking and more coding. "I'm really looking forward to that," he says.

Friday: Code That Writes Code

So far you've seen many wonderful metaprogramming spells—but it's possible that the meaning of the "m" word has only become fuzzier for you. The fact is, the original definition of metaprogramming as "writing code that writes code" doesn't fit every technique described in this book.

Rather than look for an updated, Wikipedia-worthy definition, we can accept that metaprogramming is not a single approach that you can define in a short sentence. It's more like a heterogeneous bag of tricks that all happen to revolve around the Ruby object model. And like any other bag of tricks, metaprogramming really comes into its own when you start blending many of those tricks together.

Today you'll learn a few new tricks you can add to that bag, including one that quite literally "writes code." But even better, you'll see how you can seamlessly mix and match many tricks to solve a difficult coding challenge.

Coding Your Way to the Weekend

Where your boss challenges you and Bill to write better code than she can.

After such an eventful week, you're looking forward to a relaxing Friday. But as soon as you sit down with Bill and your cup of coffee, your boss appears.

"You guys did a good job this week," she says. "Looking over your code, I got so excited about metaprogramming that I decided to learn it myself. But last night I got stuck on a difficult coding problem. Can you help me?"

Having a boss who used to be a programmer and still likes to get her hands dirty can sometimes make your life harder. But you're new at this job, and you can't say no when your boss is asking for your help.

The Boss' Challenge

A few days ago, your boss learned about the attr_accessor method that you read about in *The attr_accessor() Example*, on page 116. Now she's using attr_accessor all the time to generate her objects' attributes. While she was at it, your boss also came up with the idea of writing her own *Class Macro (117)*, similar to attr_accessor, which generates a *validated* attribute. "I call it attr_checked," she says.

Your boss explains how this attr_checked method should work, pointing out that it should take the name of the attribute, as well as a block. The block is used for validation. If you assign a value to the attribute and the block doesn't return true for that value, then you get a runtime exception.

Your boss' first requirement is an attr_checked Class Macro, and she explains her secondary requirement: "I don't want this attr_checked method to be available to each and every class, because I don't like the idea of cluttering standard classes with my own methods. Instead, a class should gain access to attr_checked only when it includes a CheckedAttributes module." She provides this example:

```
class Person
➤   include CheckedAttributes

    attr_checked :age do |v|
      v >= 18
    end
end

me = Person.new
me.age = 39      # OK
me.age = 12      # Exception
```

Your task today is to write CheckedAttributes and attr_checked for your boss.

A Development Plan

The boss' challenge is a bit too much to handle in a single burst of coding. You'll get to a solution in small steps.

Instead of engaging in pair programming, Bill proposes sharing roles: he'll manage the development, and you'll write the code. While you wonder what "managing the development" actually means, Bill quickly lists the steps you'll take:

1. Write a *Kernel Method (32)* named add_checked_attribute using eval to add a super-simple validated attribute to a class.

2. Refactor add_checked_attribute to remove eval.

3. Validate attributes through a block.

4. Change add_checked_attribute to a *Class Macro (117)* named attr_checked that's available to all classes.

5. Write a module adding attr_checked to selected classes through a hook.

"Aren't we supposed to work as a pair?" you ask. "I don't even understand these steps."

"Don't worry," Bill says. "You really only need to learn two things before you start developing: one is a method named eval, and the other is the concept of a Hook Method." He vows to tell you everything you need to know about eval, because eval is necessary for the first development step. You will deal with Hook Methods later.

Kernel#eval

Where you learn that, when it comes right down to it, code is just text.

You already learned about instance_eval and class_eval (in *instance_eval()*, on page 84, and *class_eval()*, on page 107, respectively). Now you can get acquainted with the third member of the **eval* family—a *Kernel Method (32)* that's simply named eval. Kernel#eval is the most straightforward of the three **eval* methods. Instead of a block, it takes a string that contains Ruby code—a *String of Code* for short. Kernel#eval executes the code in the string and returns the result:

Spell: String of Code, page 242

ctwc/simple_eval.rb

```
array = [10, 20]
element = 30
eval("array << element")  # => [10, 20, 30]
```

Executing a literal string of Ruby code is a pretty pointless exercise, but the power of eval becomes apparent when you compute your Strings of Code on the fly. Here's an example.

The REST Client Example

REST Client (installed with gem install rest-client) is a simple HTTP client library. It includes an interpreter where you can issue regular Ruby commands together with HTTP methods such as get:

⇒ **restclient http://www.twitter.com**

```
> html_first_chars = get("/")[0..14]
=> "<!DOCTYPE html>"
```

If you look in the gem's source, you will see that get and the three other basic HTTP methods are defined on the Resource class:

gems/rest-client-1.6.7/lib/restclient/resource.rb

```
module RestClient
  class Resource
    def get(additional_headers={}, &block) # ...
    def post(payload, additional_headers={}, &block) # ...
    def put(payload, additional_headers={}, &block) # ...
    def delete(additional_headers={}, &block) # ...
```

To make get and its siblings available in the interpreter, REST Client defines four top-level methods that delegate to the methods of a Resource at a specific URL. For example, here is how the top-level get delegates to a Resource (returned by the r method):

```
def  get(path, *args, &b)
  r[path].get(*args, &b)
end
```

You might expect to find this definition of get in the source code, together with similar definitions for put, post, and delete. However, here comes a twist. Instead of defining the four methods separately, REST Client defines all of them in one shot by creating and evaluating four *Strings of Code (141)* in a loop:

gems/rest-client-1.6.7/bin/restclient

```
POSSIBLE_VERBS = ['get', 'put', 'post', 'delete']

POSSIBLE_VERBS.each do |m|
  eval <<-end_eval
    def #{m}(path, *args, &b)
        r[path].#{m}(*args, &b)
    end
  end_eval
end
```

The code above uses an exotic syntax known as a *here document*, or *heredoc* for short. What you're seeing after the eval is just a regular Ruby string, although it's not delimited by the usual quotes. Instead, it starts with a <<-sequence followed by an arbitrary *termination sequence*—in this case, end_eval. The string ends on the first line that contains only the termination sequence, so this particular string spans the lines from the def to the first end included. The code uses regular string substitution to generate and eval four Strings of Code, one each for the definitions of get, put, post, and delete.

Most Strings of Code feature some kind of string substitution, as in the example above. For an alternate way to use eval, you can evaluate arbitrary Strings of Code from an external source, effectively building your own simple Ruby interpreter.

If you want to use Kernel#eval to its fullest potential, you should also learn about the Binding class.

Binding Objects

A Binding is a whole scope packaged as an object. The idea is that you can create a Binding to capture the local scope and carry it around. Later, you can execute code in that scope by using the Binding object in conjunction with eval.

You can create a Binding with the Kernel#binding method:

ctwc/bindings.rb

```
class MyClass
  def my_method
    @x = 1
    binding
  end
end

b = MyClass.new.my_method
```

You can think of Binding objects as "purer" forms of closures than blocks because these objects contain a scope but don't contain code. You can evaluate code in the captured scope by passing the Binding as an additional argument to eval:

```
eval "@x", b        # => 1
```

Ruby also provides a predefined constant named TOPLEVEL_BINDING, which is just a Binding of the top-level scope. You can use it to access the top-level scope from anywhere in your program:

```
class AnotherClass
  def my_method
    eval "self", TOPLEVEL_BINDING
  end
end

AnotherClass.new.my_method    # => main
```

One gem that makes good use of bindings is Pry, which you met in *The Pry Example*, on page 49. Pry defines an Object#pry method that opens an interactive session inside the object's scope, similar to what irb does with nested sessions. You can use this function as a debugger of sorts: instead of setting a breakpoint, you add a line to your code that calls pry on the current bindings, as shown in the following code.

```
# code...
require "pry"; binding.pry
```

```
# more code...
```

The call to binding.pry opens a Ruby interpreter in the current bindings, right inside the running process. From there, you can read and change your variables at will. When you want to exit the interpreter, just type exit to continue running the program. Thanks to this feature, Pry is a great alternative to traditional debuggers.

Pry is not the only command-line interpreter that uses bindings. Let's also look at irb, the default Ruby command-line utility.

The irb Example

Spell: Code Processor, page 233

At its core, irb is just a simple program that parses the standard input or a file and passes each line to eval. (This type of program is sometimes called a *Code Processor.*) Here's the line that calls eval, deep within irb's source code, in a file named workspace.rb:

```
eval(statements, @binding, file, line)
```

The statements argument is just a line of Ruby code. But what about those three additional arguments to eval? Let's go through them.

The first optional argument to eval is a Binding, and irb can change this argument to evaluate code in different contexts. This happens, for example, when you open a nested irb session on a specific object, by typing irb followed by the name of an object in an existing irb session. As a result, your next commands will be evaluated in the context of the object, similar to what instance_eval does.

What about file and line, the remaining two optional arguments to eval? These arguments are used to tweak the stack trace in case of exceptions. You can see how they work by writing a Ruby program that raises an exception:

ctwc/exception.rb

```
# this file raises an Exception on the second line
x = 1 / 0
```

You can process this program with irb by typing irb exception.rb at the prompt. If you do that, you'll get an exception on line 2 of exception.rb:

```
❮ ZeroDivisionError: divided by 0
    from exception.rb:2:in `/'
```

When irb calls eval, it calls it with the filename and line number it's currently processing. That's why you get the right information in the exception's stack trace. Just for fun, you can hack irb's source and remove the last two arguments from the call to eval (remember to undo the change afterward):

```
eval(statements, @binding) # , file, line)
```

Run irb exception.rb now, and the exception reports the file and line where eval is called:

```
ZeroDivisionError: divided by 0
    from /Users/nusco/.rvm/rubies/ruby-2.0.0/lib/ruby/2.0.0/irb/workspace.rb:54:in `/'
```

This kind of hacking of the stack trace is especially useful when you write Code Processors—but consider using it everywhere you evaluate a *String of Code (141)* so you can get a better stack trace in case of an exception.

Strings of Code vs. Blocks

In *Kernel#eval*, on page 141, you learned that eval is a special case in the eval* family: it evaluates a *String of Code (141)* instead of a block, like both class_eval and instance_eval do. However, this is not the whole truth. Although it's true that eval always requires a string, instance_eval and class_eval can take either a String of Code or a block.

This shouldn't come as a big surprise. After all, code in a string is not that different from code in a block. Strings of Code can even access local variables like blocks do:

```
array = ['a', 'b', 'c']
x = 'd'
array.instance_eval "self[1] = x"

array    # => ["a", "d", "c"]
```

Because a block and a String of Code are so similar, in many cases you have the option of using either one. Which one should you choose? The short answer is that you should probably avoid Strings of Code whenever you have an alternative. Let's see why.

The Trouble with eval()

Strings of Code are powerful, no doubt about that. But with great power comes great responsibility—and danger.

To start with, Strings of Code don't always play well with your editor's syntax coloring and autocompletion. Even when they *do* get along with everyone, Strings of Code tend to be difficult to read and modify. Also, Ruby won't report a syntax error in a String of Code until that string is evaluated, potentially resulting in brittle programs that fail unexpectedly at runtime.

Thankfully, these annoyances are minor compared to the biggest issue with eval: security. This particular problem calls for a more detailed explanation.

Code Injection

Assume that, like most people, you have trouble remembering what each of the umpteen methods of Array does. As a speedy way to refresh your memory, you can write an eval-based utility that allows you to call a method on a sample array and view the result (call it the *array explorer*):

`ctwc/array_explorer.rb`

```ruby
def explore_array(method)
  code = "['a', 'b', 'c'].#{method}"
  puts "Evaluating: #{code}"
  eval code
end

loop { p explore_array(gets.chomp()) }
```

The infinite loop on the last line collects strings from the standard input and feeds these strings to explore_array. In turn, explore_array turns the strings into method calls on a sample array. For example, if you feed the string *"reverse()"* to explore_array, the method will evaluate the string *"['a', 'b', 'c'].reverse()"*. It's time to try out this utility:

```
⇒ find_index("b")
❮ Evaluating: ['a', 'b', 'c'].find_index("b")
  1
⇒ map! {|e| e.next }
❮ Evaluating: ['a', 'b', 'c'].map! {|e| e.next }
  ["b", "c", "d"]
```

Now imagine that, being a sharing kind of person, you decide to make this program widely available on the web. You hack together a quick web page, and—presto!—you have a site where people can call array methods and see the results. (To sound like a proper startup, you might call this site "Arry" or maybe "MeThood.") Your wonderful site takes the Internet by storm, until a sneaky user feeds it a string like this:

```
⇒ object_id; Dir.glob("*")
❮ ['a', 'b', 'c'].object_id; Dir.glob("*") => [your own private information here]
```

The input is an inconsequential call to the array, followed by a command that lists all the files in your program's directory. Oh, the horror! Your malicious user can now execute arbitrary code on your computer—code that does something terrible like wipe your hard disk clean or post your love letters to your entire address book. This kind of exploit is called a *code injection* attack.

Defending Yourself from Code Injection

How can you protect your code from code injection? You might parse all *Strings of Code (141)* to identify operations that are potentially dangerous. This approach may prove ineffective, though, because there are so many possible ways to write malicious code. Trying to outsmart a determined hacker can be dangerous to both your computer and your ego.

When it comes to code injection, some strings are safer than others. Only strings that derive from an external source can contain malicious code, so you might simply limit your use of eval to those strings that you wrote yourself. This is the case in *The REST Client Example*, on page 141. In more complicated cases, however, it can be surprisingly difficult to track which strings come from where.

With all these challenges, some programmers advocate banning eval altogether. Programmers tend to be paranoid about anything that might possibly go wrong, so this eval ban turns out to be a pretty popular choice. (Actually, we're not paranoid. It's the government putting something in the tap water that makes us *feel* that way.)

If you do away with eval, you'll have to look for alternative techniques on a case-by-case basis. For an example, look back at the eval in *The REST Client Example*, on page 141. You could replace it with a *Dynamic Method (51)* and *Dynamic Dispatch (48)*:

```
ctwc/rest_client_without_eval.rb
```

```ruby
POSSIBLE_VERBS.each do |m|
  define_method m do |path, *args, &b|
    r[path].send(m, *args, &b)
  end
end
```

In the same way, you could rewrite the Array Explorer utility from *Code Injection*, on page 146, by using a Dynamic Dispatch in place of eval:

```
ctwc/array_explorer_without_eval.rb
```

```ruby
def explore_array(method, *arguments)
  ['a', 'b', 'c'].send(method, *arguments)
end
```

Still, there are times when you might just miss eval. For example, this latest, safer version of the Array Explorer wouldn't allow your web user to call a method that takes a block. If you want to describe a Ruby block in a web interface, you need to allow the user to insert arbitrary Strings of Code.

It's not easy to hit the sweet spot between too much eval and no eval at all. If you don't want to abstain from eval completely, Ruby does provide some features that make it somewhat safer. Let's take a look at them.

Tainted Objects and Safe Levels

Ruby automatically marks potentially unsafe objects—in particular, objects that come from external sources—as *tainted*. Tainted objects include strings that your program reads from web forms, files, the command line, or even a system variable. Every time you create a new string by manipulating tainted strings, the result is itself tainted. Here's an example program that checks whether an object is tainted by calling its tainted? method:

ctwc/tainted_objects.rb

```
# read user input
user_input = "User input: #{gets()}"
puts user_input.tainted?
```

⇒ x = 1
❮ true

If you had to check every string for taintedness, then you wouldn't be in a much better position than if you had simply tracked unsafe strings on your own. But Ruby also provides the notion of *safe levels*, which complement tainted objects nicely. When you set a safe level (which you can do by assigning a value to the $SAFE global variable), you disallow certain potentially dangerous operations.

You can choose from four safe levels, from the default 0 ("hippie commune," where you can hug trees and format hard disks) to 3 ("military dictatorship," where every object you create is tainted by default). A safe level of 2, for example, disallows most file-related operations. Any safe level greater than 0 also causes Ruby to flat-out refuse to evaluate tainted strings:

```
$SAFE = 1
user_input = "User input: #{gets()}"
eval user_input
```

⇒ x = 1
❮ SecurityError: Insecure operation - eval

Ruby 2.0 and earlier also had a safe level of 4 that didn't even allow you to exit the program freely. For various reasons, this extreme safe level turned out to be not as secure as people assumed it would be, so it has been removed in Ruby 2.1.

To fine-tune safety, you can explicitly remove the taintedness on Strings of Code before you evaluate them (you can do that by calling Object#untaint) and then rely on safe levels to disallow dangerous operations such as disk access.

By using safe levels carefully, you can write a controlled environment for eval. Such an environment is called a *Sandbox*. Let's take a look at a Sandbox taken from a real-life library.

Spell: Sandbox, page 240

The ERB Example

The ERB standard library is the default Ruby template system. This library is a *Code Processor (144)* that you can use to embed Ruby into any file, such as this template containing a snippet of HTML:

`ctwc/template.rhtml`

```
<p><strong>Wake up!</strong> It's a nice sunny <%= Time.new.strftime("%A") %>.</p>
```

The special <%= ... > tag contains embedded Ruby code. When you pass this template through ERB, the code is evaluated:

`ctwc/erb_example.rb`

```ruby
require 'erb'
erb = ERB.new(File.read('template.rhtml'))
erb.run
```

❮ `<p><strong>Wake up!</strong> It's a nice sunny Friday.</p>`

Somewhere in ERB's source, there must be a method that takes a snippet of Ruby code extracted from the template and passes it to eval. Sure enough, here it is:

```ruby
class ERB
  def result(b=new_toplevel)
    if @safe_level
      proc {
        $SAFE = @safe_level
        eval(@src, b, (@filename || '(erb)'), 0)
      }.call
    else
      eval(@src, b, (@filename || '(erb)'), 0)
    end
  end
  #...
```

new_toplevel is a method that returns a copy of TOPLEVEL_BINDING. The @src instance variable carries the content of a code tag, and the @safe_level instance variable contains the safe level required by the user. If no safe level is set, the content of the tag is simply evaluated. Otherwise, ERB builds a quick *Sandbox (149)*:

it makes sure that the global safe level is exactly what the user asked for and also uses a Proc as a *Clean Room (87)* to execute the code in a separate scope. (Note that the new value of $SAFE applies only inside the Proc. Contrary to what happens with other global variables, the Ruby interpreter takes care to reset $SAFE to its former value after the call.)

"Now," Bill says, finally wrapping up his long explanation, "you know about eval and how dangerous it can be. But eval is great to get code up and running quickly. That's why you can use this method as a first step to solve your original problem: writing the attribute generator for the boss."

Kernel#eval() and Kernel#load()

Ruby has methods like Kernel#load and Kernel#require that take the name of a source file and execute code from that file. If you think about it, evaluating a file is not that different from evaluating a string. This means load and require are somewhat similar to eval. Although these methods are not really part of the *eval family, you can think of them as first cousins.

You can usually control the content of your files, so you don't have as many security concerns with load and require as you do with eval. Still, safe levels higher than 1 do put some limitations on importing files. For example, a safe level of 2 or higher prevents you from using load with a tainted filename.

Quiz: Checked Attributes (Step 1)

Where you take your first step toward solving the boss' challenge, with Bill looking over your shoulder.

You and Bill look back at the first two steps of your development plan:

1. Write a *Kernel Method (32)* named add_checked_attribute using eval to add a super-simple validated attribute to a class.

2. Refactor add_checked_attribute to remove eval.

Focus on the first step. The add_checked_attribute method should generate a reader method and a writer method, pretty much like attr_accessor does. However, add_checked_attribute should differ from attr_accessor in three ways. First, while attr_accessor is a *Class Macro (117)*, add_checked_attribute is supposed to be a simple *Kernel Method (32)*. Second, attr_accessor is written in C, while add_checked_attribute should use plain Ruby (and a *String of Code (141)*). Finally, add_checked_attribute should add one basic example of validation to the attribute: the attribute will raise a runtime exception if you assign it either nil or false. (You'll deal with flexible validation down the road.)

These requirements are expressed more clearly in a test suite:

ctwc/checked_attributes/eval.rb

```ruby
require 'test/unit'

class Person; end

class TestCheckedAttribute < Test::Unit::TestCase
  def setup
    add_checked_attribute(Person, :age)
    @bob = Person.new
  end

  def test_accepts_valid_values
    @bob.age = 20
    assert_equal 20, @bob.age
  end

  def test_refuses_nil_values
    assert_raises RuntimeError, 'Invalid attribute' do
      @bob.age = nil
    end
  end

  def test_refuses_false_values
    assert_raises RuntimeError, 'Invalid attribute' do
      @bob.age = false
    end
  end
end

# Here is the method that you should implement.
def add_checked_attribute(klass, attribute)
  # ...
end
```

(The reference to the class in add_checked_attribute is called klass because class is a reserved word in Ruby.)

Can you implement add_checked_attribute and pass the test?

Before You Solve This Quiz...

You need to generate an attribute like attr_accessor does. You might appreciate a short review of attr_accessor, which we talked about first in *The attr_accessor()* *Example*, on page 116. When you tell attr_accessor that you want an attribute named, say, :my_attr, it generates two *Mimic Methods (218)* like the following:

```ruby
def my_attr
  @my_attr
end

def my_attr=(value)
  @my_attr = value
end
```

Quiz Solution

Here's a solution:

```ruby
def add_checked_attribute(klass, attribute)
  eval "
    class #{klass}
      def #{attribute}=(value)
        raise 'Invalid attribute' unless value
        @#{attribute} = value
      end

      def #{attribute}()
        @#{attribute}
      end
    end
  "
end
```

Here's the *String of Code (141)* that gets evaluated when you call add_checked_attribute(String, :my_attr):

```ruby
class String
  def my_attr=(value)
    raise 'Invalid attribute' unless value
    @my_attr = value
  end

  def my_attr()
    @my_attr
  end
end
```

The String class is treated as an *Open Class (14)*, and it gets two new methods. These methods are almost identical to those that would be generated by attr_accessor, with an additional check that raises an exception if you call my_attr= with either nil or false.

"That was a good start," Bill says. "But remember our plan. We only used eval to pass the unit tests quickly; we don't want to stick with eval for the real solution. This takes us to step 2."

Quiz: Checked Attributes (Step 2)

Where you make your code eval-free.

You glance at the development plan. Your next step is refactoring add_checked_attribute and replacing eval with regular Ruby methods.

You may be wondering why the obsession with removing eval. How can add_checked_attribute be a target for a code injection attack if it's meant to be used only by you and your teammates? The problem is, you never know whether this method might be exposed to the world some time in the future. Besides, if you rewrite the same method without using *Strings of Code (141)*, it will only get clearer and more elegant for human readers, and less confusing for tools like syntax higlighters. These considerations are reason enough to go forward and drop eval altogether.

Can you refactor add_checked_attribute with the same method signature and the same unit tests but using standard Ruby methods in place of eval? Be forewarned that to solve this quiz, you'll have to do some research. You'll probably need to dig through the Ruby standard libraries for methods that can replace the operations in the current String of Code. You'll also need to manage scope carefully so that the attribute is defined in the context of the right class. (Hint: remember *Flat Scopes (83)?*)

Quiz Solution

To define methods in a class, you need to get into that class's scope. The previous version of add_checked_attribute did that by using an *Open Class (14)* inside a String of Code. If you remove eval, you cannot use the class keyword anymore, because class won't accept a variable for the class name. Instead, you can get into the class's scope with class_eval.

ctwc/checked_attributes/no_eval.rb

```
def add_checked_attribute(klass, attribute)
➤   klass.class_eval do
➤     # ...
➤   end
end
```

You're in the class now, and you can define the reader and writer methods. Previously, you did that by using the def keyword in the String of Code. Again, you can no longer use def, because you won't know the names of the methods until runtime. In place of def, you can use *Dynamic Methods (51)*:

```
def add_checked_attribute(klass, attribute)
  klass.class_eval do
```

```
➤        define_method "#{attribute}=" do |value|
➤          # ...
➤        end
➤
➤        define_method attribute do
➤          # ...
➤        end
      end
    end
```

The previous code defines two *Mimic Methods (218)* that are supposed to read and write an instance variable. How can the code do this without evaluating a String of Code? If you browse through Ruby's documentation, you'll find a few methods that manipulate instance variables, including Object#instance_variable_get and Object#instance_variable_set. Let's use them:

```
def add_checked_attribute(klass, attribute)
  klass.class_eval do
    define_method "#{attribute}=" do |value|
➤      raise 'Invalid attribute' unless value
➤      instance_variable_set("@#{attribute}", value)
    end

    define_method attribute do
➤      instance_variable_get "@#{attribute}"
    end
  end
end
```

"That's it," Bill says. "We now have a method that enters a class scope and defines instance methods that manipulate instance variables, and there's no string-based eval to speak of. Now that our code is both working and eval-free, we can move on to the third step in our development plan."

Quiz: Checked Attributes (Step 3)

Where you sprinkle some flexibility over today's project.

To solve the boss' challenge, you and Bill still need to implement a few important features. One of these features is described in the third step of your development plan: "validate attributes through a block." Right now, your generated attribute raises an exception if you assign it nil or false. But it's supposed to support flexible validation through a block.

Because this step changes the interface of add_checked_attribute, it also calls for an update of the test suite. Bill replaces the two test cases that checked for nil or false attributes with a single new test case:

ctwc/checked_attributes/block.rb

```ruby
require 'test/unit'

class Person; end

class TestCheckedAttribute < Test::Unit::TestCase
  def setup
➤    add_checked_attribute(Person, :age) { |v| v >= 18 }
    @bob = Person.new
  end

  def test_accepts_valid_values
    @bob.age = 20
    assert_equal 20, @bob.age
  end

➤  def test_refuses_invalid_values
➤    assert_raises RuntimeError, 'Invalid attribute' do
➤      @bob.age = 17
➤    end
➤  end
end

➤ def add_checked_attribute(klass, attribute, &validation)
  # ... (The code here doesn't pass the test. Modify it.)
end
```

Can you modify add_checked_attribute so that it passes the new tests?

Quiz Solution

You can pass the tests and solve the quiz by changing a couple of lines in add_checked_attribute:

```ruby
➤ def add_checked_attribute(klass, attribute, &validation)
  klass.class_eval do
    define_method "#{attribute}=" do |value|
➤      raise 'Invalid attribute' unless validation.call(value)
      instance_variable_set("@#{attribute}", value)
    end

    define_method attribute do
      instance_variable_get "@#{attribute}"
    end
  end
end
```

"Step 3 was quick," Bill notes. "Let's move on to step 4."

Quiz: Checked Attributes (Step 4)

Where you pull a Class Macro (117) from your bag of tricks.

The fourth step in your development plan asks you to change the Kernel Method to a *Class Macro (117)* that's available to all classes.

What this means is that instead of an add_checked_attribute method, you want an attr_checked method that the boss can use in a class definition. Also, instead of taking a class and an attribute name, this new method should take only the attribute name, because the class is already available as self.

Bill updates the test case:

ctwc/checked_attributes/macro.rb

```ruby
require 'test/unit'

class Person
➤   attr_checked :age do |v|
➤     v >= 18
➤   end
end

class TestCheckedAttributes < Test::Unit::TestCase
  def setup
➤     @bob = Person.new
  end

  def test_accepts_valid_values
    @bob.age = 20
    assert_equal 20, @bob.age
  end

  def test_refuses_invalid_values
    assert_raises RuntimeError, 'Invalid attribute' do
      @bob.age = 17
    end
  end
end
```

Can you write the attr_checked method and pass the tests?

Quiz Solution

Think back to the discussion of class definitions in *Class Definitions Demystified*, on page 106. If you want to make attr_checked available to any class definition, you can simply make it an instance method of either Class or Module. Let's go for the first option:

ctwc/checked_attributes/macro.rb

```ruby
➤ class Class
➤   def attr_checked(attribute, &validation)
    define_method "#{attribute}=" do |value|
      raise 'Invalid attribute' unless validation.call(value)
      instance_variable_set("@#{attribute}", value)
```

```
    end
    define_method attribute do
      instance_variable_get "@#{attribute}"
    end
  end
end
```

This code doesn't even need to call to class_eval, because when the method executes, the class is already taking the role of self.

"That's great," Bill says. "One more step, and we'll be done." For this last step, however, you need to learn about a feature that we haven't talked about yet: Hook Methods.

Hook Methods

Where you get one of Bill's thorough lessons in advanced coding.

The object model is an eventful place. Lots of things happen there as your code runs: classes are inherited, modules are mixed into classes, and methods are defined, undefined, and removed. Imagine if you could "catch" these events like you catch GUI mouse-click events. You'd be able to execute code whenever a class is inherited or whenever a class gains a new method.

Well, it turns out you can do all these things. This program prints a notification on the screen when a class inherits from String:

ctwc/hooks.rb
```
class String
  def self.inherited(subclass)
    puts "#{self} was inherited by #{subclass}"
  end
end

class MyString < String; end
```

❮ String was inherited by MyString

The inherited method is an instance method of Class, and Ruby calls it when a class is inherited. By default, Class#inherited does nothing, but you can override it with your own code as in the earlier example. A method such as Class#inherited is called a *Hook Method* because you can use it to hook into a particular event.

Spell: Hook Method, page 236

More Hooks

Ruby provides a motley bunch of hooks that cover the most newsworthy events in the object model. Just as you override Class#inherited to plug into the lifecycle of classes, you can plug into the lifecycle of modules by overriding Module#included and (in Ruby 2.0) Module#prepended:

```ruby
module M1
  def self.included(othermod)
    puts "M1 was included into #{othermod}"
  end
end

module M2
  def self.prepended(othermod)
    puts "M2 was prepended to #{othermod}"
  end
end

class C
  include M1
  prepend M2
end
```

```
❰ M1 was included into C
  M2 was prepended to C
```

You can also execute code when a module extends an object by overriding Module#extended. Finally, you can execute method-related events by overriding Module#method_added, method_removed, or method_undefined.

```ruby
module M
  def self.method_added(method)
    puts "New method: M##{method}"
  end

  def my_method; end
end
```

```
❰ New method: M#my_method
```

These hooks only work for regular instance methods, which live in the object's class. They don't work for *Singleton Methods (115)*, which live in the object's singleton class. To catch Singleton Method events, you can use BasicObject#singleton_method_added, singleton_method_removed, and singleton_method_undefined.

Module#included is probably the most widely used hook, thanks to a common metaprogramming spell that's worthy of an example of its own.

Plugging into Standard Methods

The notion of hooks extends beyond specialized methods like Class#inherited or Module#method_added. Because most operations in Ruby are just regular methods, you can easily twist them into improvised Hook Methods.

For example, in *Hook Methods*, on page 157, you learned how to override Module#included to execute code when a module is included. But you can also plug into the same event, so to speak, from the other side: because you include a module with the include method, instead of overriding Module#included, you can override Module#include itself.

For example:

```ruby
module M; end

class C
  def self.include(*modules)
    puts "Called: C.include(#{modules})"
    super
  end

  include M
end
```

```
❮ Called: C.include(M)
```

There is an important difference between overriding Module#included and overriding Module#include. Module#included exists solely to be used as a Hook Method, and its default implementation is empty. But Module#include has some real work to do: it must actually include the module. That's why our hook's code also should call the base implementation of Module#include through super. If you forget super, you'll still catch the event, but you won't include the module anymore.

As an alternative to overriding, you can turn a regular method into a Hook Method by using an *Around Alias (134)*. You can find an example of this technique in *The Thor Example*, on page 133.

The VCR Example

VCR is a gem that records and replays HTTP calls. The Request class in VCR includes a Normalizers::Body module:

```ruby
module VCR
  class Request #...
    include Normalizers::Body
    #...
```

The Body module defines methods that deal with an HTTP message body, such as body_from. After the include, those methods become class methods on Request. Yes, you read that right: Request is gaining new class methods by including Normalizers::Body. But a class usually gets *instance* methods by including a module—not *class* methods. How can a mixin like Normalizers::Body bend the rules and define class methods on its includer?

Look for the answer in the definition of the Body module itself:

gems/vcr-2.5.0/lib/vcr/structs.rb

```ruby
module VCR
  module Normalizers
    module Body
      def self.included(klass)
        klass.extend ClassMethods
      end

      module ClassMethods
        def body_from(hash_or_string)
          # ...
```

The code above pulls off a convoluted trick. Body has an inner module named ClassMethods that defines body_from and other methods as regular instance methods. Body also has an included *Hook Method (157)*. When Request includes Body, it triggers a chain of events:

- Ruby calls the included hook on Body.

- The hook turns back to Request and extends it with the ClassMethods module.

- The extend method includes the methods from ClassMethods in the Request's singleton class. (You might remember this last part of the trick from *Quiz: Module Trouble*, on page 129.)

As a result, body_from and other instance methods get mixed into the singleton class of Request, effectively becoming class methods of Request. How's that for a complicated code concoction?

This ClassMethods-plus-hook idiom used to be quite common, and it was used extensively by the Rails source code. As you'll see in Chapter 10, *Active Support's Concern Module*, on page 179, Rails has since moved to an alternate mechanism—but you can still find examples of the idiom in VCR and other gems.

Quiz: Checked Attributes (Step 5)

Where you finally earn Bill's respect and the title of Master of Metaprogramming.

The following is the code that we wrote in the previous development step:

```ruby
class Class
  def attr_checked(attribute, &validation)
    define_method "#{attribute}=" do |value|
      raise 'Invalid attribute' unless validation.call(value)
      instance_variable_set("@#{attribute}", value)
    end

    define_method attribute do
      instance_variable_get "@#{attribute}"
    end
  end
end
```

This code defines a *Class Macro (117)* named attr_checked. This Class Macro is an instance method of Class, so it's available to all classes. The final step in your development plan asks you to restrict access to attr_checked: it should be available only to those classes that include a module named CheckedAttributes. The test suite for this step is pretty much the same one you used in step 4, with a single additional line:

ctwc/checked_attributes/module.rb

```ruby
require 'test/unit'

class Person
➤  include CheckedAttributes

  attr_checked :age do |v|
    v >= 18
  end
end

class TestCheckedAttributes < Test::Unit::TestCase
  def setup
    @bob = Person.new
  end

  def test_accepts_valid_values
    @bob.age = 18
    assert_equal 18, @bob.age
  end

  def test_refuses_invalid_values
    assert_raises RuntimeError, 'Invalid attribute' do
      @bob.age = 17
    end
  end
end
```

Can you remove attr_checked from Class, write the CheckedAttributes module, and solve the boss' challenge?

Quiz Solution

You can copy the trick that you learned in *The VCR Example*, on page 159.
CheckedAttributes defines attr_checked as a class method on its includers:

```
module CheckedAttributes
  def self.included(base)
    base.extend ClassMethods
  end

  module ClassMethods
    def attr_checked(attribute, &validation)
      define_method "#{attribute}=" do |value|
        raise 'Invalid attribute' unless validation.call(value)
        instance_variable_set("@#{attribute}", value)
      end

      define_method attribute do
        instance_variable_get "@#{attribute}"
      end
    end
  end
end
```

Your boss will be delighted. These are the same Class Macro and module that
she challenged you to write this morning. If you can write code like this, you're
on your way to mastering the art of metaprogramming.

Wrap-Up

Today you solved a difficult metaprogramming problem, writing your own
useful *Class Macro (117)*. Along the way, you also learned about the powerful
eval method, its issues, and how to work around them. Finally, you got introduced to Ruby's *Hook Methods (157)*, and you used them to your advantage.

"You learned a lot this week, my friend," Bill says, smiling for what seems
like the first time this week. "Now you know enough to walk the metaprogramming path on your own. Before we take off for the weekend, let me tell you
one last story."

"A master developer," Bill begins, "sits on top of a mountain, meditating…"

Epilogue

A master developer was meditating on top of a steep mountain. So deep was his meditation, so profoundly interwoven his code and his soul, that he began to snore gently.

A disciple climbed the mountain and interrupted the master's concentration. "I am struggling terribly, Master," he said. "I've studied many advanced techniques, but I still don't know how to apply them correctly. Tell me, what's the essence of metaprogramming?"

"Look at this small tree by my side," the master replied, languidly waving his hand. "See how delicately it bends toward the ground, as if feeding on its own roots? Thus must your code be: simple and plain, and closing in on itself like a circle."

"I am still confused, Master," said the disciple, even more worried than before. "They always taught me that self-modifying code is bad. How will I know that I am wielding this art properly?"

"Look over your code with a pure heart and a clean mind," the master coached the disciple. "You will know when the code gets obscure. Exercise your knowledge to shed light, not to obfuscate and confuse."

"But Master," the disciple argued, "I lack experience. I need simple rules to know right from wrong."

The master began to get annoyed. "You're smart enough to learn," he said, "but are you smart enough to forget what you have learned? There's no such thing as metaprogramming. It's just programming all the way down. Now get lost, and let me meditate in peace."

At those words, the disciple was enlightened.

Part II

Metaprogramming in Rails

Good artists copy, great artists steal.
> *Pablo Picasso*

CHAPTER 8

Preparing for a Rails Tour

In the first part of this book, you spent a week brushing elbows with another coder and making your way through the internals of Ruby. You also filled your toolbox with magic metaprogramming tricks, such as *Dynamic Methods (51)* and *Class Macros (117)*.

So, you've got the know-how and the tools. But now you're wondering how to combine them into real-life code. How can you keep your *Open Classes (14)* under control? When should you use a *Ghost Method (57)* rather than a *Dynamic Method (51)*? How do you test your *Class Macros (117)*? To answer these kinds of questions, you need more than knowledge and tools. You need *experience.*

You can't get experience simply by reading a book, but you *can* get a lot of value out of looking at the work of experienced coders. The short chapters in this second part of the book take you on a tour through the source code of Ruby on Rails (or just "Rails," for short), the quintessential Ruby project. Rails' code uses metaprogramming at every step and is often more complex than any code you've seen so far in this book. Because of that complexity, it's a great example of both the power of metaprogramming and its potential dangers.

Rather than an exhaustive exploration of Rails, this tour is like a sightseeing excursion on one of those open-air, double-decker buses. I'll trace a few scenic routes through the Rails source code, and in the process show you how some of the best Ruby programmers apply metaprogramming spells to solve real-life problems. But first, let's talk about Rails itself.

Ruby on Rails

Chances are, you already know that Rails is a framework for developing database-backed web applications in Ruby. Rails is so popular that many people get into Ruby just so that they can use Rails.

Even if you don't know much about Rails and its features, you can still follow along on this tour. We'll focus on the Rails source code, not on the features. Whenever features *are* important to understand the source code, I'll take the time to demonstrate them. Although you don't have to, you might want to get a quick introduction to Rails on its official site[1] if you're completely new to it.

While touring the Rails source code, I'll show you the snippets of code I want to focus on. However, you might also want to keep the source code handy to explore it on your own. To do that, you need to install Rails.

Installing Rails

Because Rails is always evolving, it's quite possible that the source code will have changed significantly by the time you read this chapter. Luckily, you can easily install the same version of Rails that I used to write this book, by typing gem install rails -v 4.1.0.

Some of the next few chapters also discuss code from a much older version of Rails, to show you how Rails' source code has evolved over time. If you wish, you can install this older version alongside the more recent one, by typing gem install rails -v 2.3.2.

Running the commands above installs all the gems that make up Rails 4.1.0 and 2.3.2. The rails gem just contains helpers, such as code generators and Rake tasks, as well as the glue code that binds together the other gems. Those other gems are the ones that do the real work. Three of the most important ones are activerecord (which maps application objects to database tables), actionpack (which deals with the "web" part of the web framework), and activesupport (which contains utilities for generic problems, such as time calculations and logging).

The Rails Source Code

When referring to a specific source file, I'll give you the file's path inside the system's gems directory, such as gems/activerecord-4.1.0/lib/active_record.rb. If you want to explore on your own, you can use RubyGem's unpack command to

---

1.   http://rubyonrails.org

access Rails' entire source code with a minimum of fuss. For example, gem unpack activerecord -v=4.1.0 will copy the entire distribution of Active Record 4.1.0 to the current directory.

As of version 4, Rails and its core libraries contain almost 170,000 lines of code (including white lines and comments). You can cram a lot of information into just a few lines of Ruby code—let alone hundreds of thousands. Also, you can barely find a Rails source file that doesn't make heavy use of metaprogramming spells and other sophisticated idioms and techniques. All things considered, the Rails source code contains enough information to be intimidating.

These challenges shouldn't stop you from browsing through this wonderful code. The Rails source code can be daunting, but it's also chock full of interesting metaprogramming tricks. Start slowly, don't get discouraged as you piece together the basics, and soon you might enter the growing list of Rails contributors.

Also, don't forget the unit tests. When you're confronted with a confusing piece of code, reach for its tests and find out how it's supposed to be used. Once you understand their intention, most perplexing lines of code will suddenly make sense.

Now you have the Rails source code and the tools you need to explore it. In the next chapter, we'll dive into the first stop on our tour: a quick look at Active Record, the most iconic of the Rails components.

The Design of Active Record

Active Record is the library in Rails that maps Ruby objects to database records. This functionality is called *object-relational mapping*, and it allows you to get the best of both the relational database (used for persistence) and object-oriented programming (used for business logic).

In this chapter, as well as the next two, we'll take a look at the high-level design of Active Record's source code and how its pieces fit together. We are less interested in *what* Active Record does than *how* it does it. All we need is a very short example of mapping a class to a database—just enough to kick-start our exploration of Active Record's internals.

A Short Active Record Example

Assume that you already have a file-based SQLite database that follows Active Record's conventions: this database contains a table called ducks, which has a field called name. You want to map the records in the ducks table to objects of class Duck in your code.

Let's start by requiring Active Record and opening a connection to the database. (If you want to run this code on your system, you also need to install the SQLite database and the sqlite3 gem. But you can probably follow along fine by just reading the example, without running it.)

part2/ar_example.rb

```
require 'active_record'
ActiveRecord::Base.establish_connection :adapter => "sqlite3",
                                        :database => "dbfile"
```

Note that in a Rails application, you don't need to worry about opening the connection; the application reads the names of the adapter and the database from a configuration file, and it calls establish_connection for you. We're using Active Record on its own here, so we have to open the connection ourselves.

ActiveRecord::Base is the most important class in Active Record. Not only does it contain class methods that do important things, such as opening database connections, it's also the superclass of all mapped classes, such as Duck:

```
class Duck < ActiveRecord::Base
  validate do
    errors.add(:base, "Illegal duck name.") unless name[0] == 'D'
  end
end
```

The validate method is a *Class Macro (117)* that takes a block. You don't have to worry about the details of the code in the block—just know that in this example, it ensures that a Duck's name begins with a D. (Our company's duck-naming policies demand that.) If you try to save a Duck with an illegal name to the database, the save! method will raise an exception, while the more discreet save will fail silently.

By convention, Active Record automatically maps Duck objects to the ducks table. By looking at the database schema, Active Record also finds out that Ducks have a name, and it defines a *Ghost Method (57)* to access that field. Thanks to these conventions, you can use the Duck class right away:

```
my_duck = Duck.new
my_duck.name = "Donald"
my_duck.valid?          # => true
my_duck.save!
```

I've checked that my_duck is valid (it begins with a D) and saved it to the database. Reading it back, you get this:

```
duck_from_database = Duck.first
duck_from_database.name          # => "Donald"
duck_from_database.delete
```

That's enough code for now to give you a sense of how Active Record is meant to be used. Now let's see what's happening under the hood.

How Active Record Is Put Together

The code in the previous example looks simple, but ActiveRecord::Base is capable of much more than that. Indeed, the more you use Active Record, the more the methods in Base seem to multiply. You might assume that Base is a huge class with thousands of lines of code that define methods such as save or validate.

Surprisingly, the source code of ActiveRecord::Base contains no trace of those methods. This is a common problem for newcomers to Rails: it's often difficult to understand where a specific method comes from and how it gets into a class such as Base. The rest of this short chapter will look at how ActiveRecord::Base's functionality is assembled.

Let's start by taking a step back to the first line in our example: require 'active_record'.

The Autoloading Mechanism

Here's the code in active_record.rb, the only Active Record file that you're likely to require:

gems/activerecord-4.1.0/lib/active_record.rb

```
require 'active_support'
require 'active_model'
# ...

module ActiveRecord
  extend ActiveSupport::Autoload

  autoload :Base
  autoload :NoTouching
  autoload :Persistence
  autoload :QueryCache
  autoload :Querying
  autoload :Validations
  # ...
```

Active Record relies heavily on two other libraries that it loads straight away: Active Support and Active Model. We'll get to Active Model soon, but one piece of Active Support is already used in this code: the ActiveSupport::Autoload module, which defines an autoload method. This method uses a naming convention to automatically find and require the source code of a module (or class) the first time you use the module's name. Active Record extends ActiveSupport::Autoload, so autoload becomes a class method on the ActiveRecord module itself. (If you're confused by this mechanism, look back at the *Class Extension (130)* spell.)

Active Record then uses autoload as a *Class Macro (117)* to register dozens of modules, a few of which you can see in the code above. As a result, Active Record acts like a smart *Namespace (23)* that automatically loads all the bits and pieces that make up the library. For example, when you use ActiveRecord::Base for the first time, autoload automatically requires the file active_record/base.rb, which in turn defines the class. Let's take a look at this definition.

ActiveRecord::Base

Here is the entire definition of ActiveRecord::Base:

gems/activerecord-4.1.0/lib/active_record/base.rb

```ruby
module ActiveRecord
  class Base
    extend ActiveModel::Naming
    extend ActiveSupport::Benchmarkable
    extend ActiveSupport::DescendantsTracker
    extend ConnectionHandling
    extend QueryCache::ClassMethods
    extend Querying
    extend Translation
    extend DynamicMatchers
    extend Explain
    extend Enum
    extend Delegation::DelegateCache

    include Core
    include Persistence
    include NoTouching
    include ReadonlyAttributes
    include ModelSchema
    include Inheritance
    include Scoping
    include Sanitization
    include AttributeAssignment
    include ActiveModel::Conversion
    include Integration
    include Validations
    include CounterCache
    include Locking::Optimistic
    include Locking::Pessimistic
    include AttributeMethods
    include Callbacks
    include Timestamp
    include Associations
    include ActiveModel::SecurePassword
    include AutosaveAssociation
    include NestedAttributes
    include Aggregations
    include Transactions
    include Reflection
    include Serialization
    include Store
    include Core
  end

  ActiveSupport.run_load_hooks(:active_record, Base)
end
```

It's not uncommon to see a class that assembles its functionality out of modules, but ActiveRecord::Base does this on a large scale. The code above does nothing but extend or include tens of modules. (Plus one additional line, the call to run_load_hooks, that allows some of those modules to run their own configuration code after they've been autoloaded.) As it turns out, many of the modules included by Base also include even more modules.

This is where the autoloading mechanism pays off. ActiveRecord::Base doesn't need to require a module's source code and then include the module. Instead, it just includes the module. Thanks to autoloading, classes such as Base can do lots of module inclusions with minimal code.

In some cases, it's not too hard to find which module a specific method in Base comes from. For example, persistence methods such as save come from ActiveRecord::Persistence:

gems/activerecord-4.1.0/lib/active_record/persistence.rb

```
module ActiveRecord
  module Persistence
    def save(*)   # ...
    def save!(*)  # ...
    def delete    # ...
```

Other method definitions are harder to find. In *A Short Active Record Example*, on page 171, you looked at validation methods such as valid? and validate. Let's go hunting for them.

The Validations Modules

Among the other modules, ActiveRecord::Base includes a module named ActiveRecord::Validations. This module looks like a good candidate to define methods such as valid? and validate. Indeed, if you look in ActiveRecord::Validations, you'll find the definition of valid?—but no validate:

gems/activerecord-4.1.0/lib/active_record/validations.rb

```
module ActiveRecord
  module Validations
    include ActiveModel::Validations
    # ...
    def valid?(context = nil) # ...
```

Where is validate? We can look for the answer in ActiveModel::Validations, a module that ActiveRecord::Validations includes. This module comes from Active Model, a library that Active Record depends on. Sure enough, if you look into its source, you'll find that validate is defined in ActiveModel::Validations.

A couple of puzzling details exist in this sequence of module inclusions. The first one is this: normally, a class gains *instance methods* by including a module. But validate is a *class method* on ActiveRecord::Base. How can Base gain class methods by including modules? This is the topic of the next chapter, *Active Support's Concern Module*, where we'll also look at the metaprogramming treasure trove that hides behind this assembly of modules. For now, notice that the modules in Active Record are special. You gain both instance *and* class methods by including them.

You might also have this question: why does ActiveRecord::Base need both ActiveRecord::Validations and ActiveModel::Validations? There is a story behind these two similarly named modules: in earlier versions of Rails there was no Active Model library, and validate was indeed defined in ActiveRecord::Validations. As Active Record kept growing, its authors realized that it was doing two separate jobs. The first job was dealing with the database operations, such as saving and loading. The second job was dealing with the object model: maintaining an object's attributes, or tracking which of those attributes were valid.

At this point, the authors of Active Record decided to split the library in two separate libraries, and thus was Active Model born. While the database-related operations stayed in Active Record, the model-related ones moved to Active Model. In particular, the valid? method has its own reasons to dabble with the database (it cares whether an object has ever been saved to the database already)—so it stayed in ActiveRecord::Validations. On the contrary, validate has no relationship to the database, and it only cares about the object's attributes. So it moved to ActiveModel::Validations.

We could hunt for more method definitions, but by now you can see what Active Record's high-level design boils down to: the most important class, ActiveRecord::Base, is an assembly of modules. Each module adds instance methods (and even class methods) to the Base mix. Some modules, such as Validations, in turn include more modules, sometimes from different libraries, bringing even more methods into Base.

Before looking deeper into Active Record's structure, let's see what this unusual design can teach us.

A Lesson Learned

By including so many modules, ActiveRecord::Base ends up being a very large class. In a plain-vanilla Rails installation, Base has more than 300 instance methods and a staggering 550 class methods. ActiveRecord::Base is the ultimate *Open Class (14)*.

When I looked at Active Record for the first time, I'd been a Java programmer for years. Active Record's source code left me shocked. No sane Java coder would ever write a library that consists almost exclusively of a single huge class with many hundreds of methods. Such a library would be madness—impossible to understand and maintain!

And yet, that's exactly what Active Record's design is like: most methods in the library ultimately get rolled inside one class. But wait, it gets worse. As we'll discuss later, some of the modules that comprise Active Record don't think twice about using metaprogramming to define even more methods on their includer. To add insult to injury, even additional libraries that work with Active Record often take the liberty of extending ActiveRecord::Base with modules and methods of their own. You might think that the result of this relentless piling up of methods would be a tangled mass of spaghetti. But it isn't.

Consider the evidence: not only does Active Record get away with that design, it also proves easy to read and change. Many users modify and *Monkeypatch (16)* Active Record for their own purposes, and hundreds of contributors have worked on the original source code. Still, the source code evolves so quickly that the poor authors of books such as this one need to rewrite most of their content with every new edition. Active Record manages to stay stable and reliable even as it changes, and most coders are happy using the latest version of the library in their production systems.

Here is the most important guideline I learned from Active Record's design: *design techniques are relative*, and they depend on the language you're using. In Ruby, you use idioms that are different from those of other languages you might be used to. It's not that the good design rules of old suddenly grew obsolete. On the contrary, the basic tenets of design (decoupling, simplicity, no duplication) hold true in Ruby as much as they do in any other language. In Ruby, though, the techniques you wield to achieve those design goals can be surprisingly different.

Look at ActiveRecord::Base again. It's a huge class, but this complex class doesn't exist in the source code. Instead, it is composed at runtime by assembling loosely coupled, easy-to-test, easy-to-reuse modules. If you only need the validation features, you can include ActiveModel::Validations in your own class and happily ignore ActiveRecord::Base and all the other modules, as in the following code:

part2/validations.rb

```ruby
require 'active_model'

class User
  include ActiveModel::Validations

  attr_accessor :password

  validate do
    errors.add(:base, "Don't let dad choose the password.") if password == '1234'
  end
end

user = User.new
user.password = '12345'
user.valid?          # => true

user.password = '1234'
user.valid?          # => false
```

Look at how well-decoupled the code above is. ActiveModel::Validations doesn't force you to meddle with inheritance, to worry about database-related concerns, or to manage any other complicated dependency. Just by including it, you get a complete set of validation methods without adding complexity.

Speaking of ActiveModel::Validations, I promised that I'd show you how this module adds class methods such as validate to its includer. I'll keep that promise in the next chapter.

Active Support's Concern Module

In the previous chapter, you saw that the modules in Rails are special: when you include them, you gain both instance and class methods. How does that happen?

The answer comes from yet another module: Concern, in the Active Support library. ActiveSupport::Concern twists and bends the Ruby object model. It encapsulates the "add class methods to your includer" functionality, and it makes it easy to roll that functionality into other modules.

ActiveSupport::Concern is easier to understand if you know how it came to exist in the first place. We'll start by looking back at Rails' older versions, before Concern entered the scene.

Rails Before Concern

The Rails source code has changed a lot through the years, but some basic ideas haven't changed much. One of these is the concept behind ActiveRecord::Base. As you've seen in *ActiveRecord::Base*, this class is an assembly of dozens of modules that define both instance methods and class methods. For example, Base includes ActiveRecord::Validations, and in the process it gets instance and class methods.

The mechanism that rolls those methods into Base, however, has changed. Let's see how it worked in the beginning.

The Include-and-Extend Trick

Around the times of Rails 2, all validation methods were defined in ActiveRecord::Validations. (Back then, there was no Active Model library.) However, Validations pulled a peculiar trick:

gems/activerecord-2.3.2/lib/active_record/validations.rb

```ruby
module ActiveRecord
  module Validations
    # ...

    def self.included(base)
      base.extend ClassMethods
      # ...
    end

    module ClassMethods
      def validates_length_of(*attrs) # ...
      # ...
    end

    def valid?
      # ...
    end

    # ...
  end
end
```

Does the code above look familiar? You've already seen this technique in *The VCR Example*, on page 159. Here's a quick recap. When ActiveRecord::Base includes Validations, three things happen:

1. The instance methods of Validations, such as valid?, become instance methods of Base. This is just regular module inclusion.

2. Ruby calls the included *Hook Method (157)* on Validations, passing ActiveRecord::Base as an argument. (The argument of included is also called base, but that name has nothing to do with the Base class—instead, it comes from the fact that a module's includer is sometimes called "the base class.")

3. The hook extends Base with the ActiveRecord::Validations::ClassMethods module. This is a *Class Extensions (130)*, so the methods in ClassMethods become class methods on Base.

As a result, Base gets both instance methods like valid? and class methods like validates_length_of.

This idiom is so specific that I hesitate to call it a spell. I'll refer to it as the *include-and-extend* trick. VCR borrowed it from Rails, as did many other Ruby projects throughout the years. Include-and-extend gives you a powerful way to structure a library: each module contains a well-isolated piece of functionality that you can roll into your classes with a simple include. That functionality can be implemented with instance methods, class methods, or both.

As clever as it is, include-and-extend has its own share of problems. For one, each and every module that defines class methods must also define a similar included hook that extends its includer. In a large codebase such as Rails', that hook was replicated over dozens of modules. As a result, people often questioned whether include-and-extend was worth the effort. After all, they observed, you can get the same result by adding one line of code to the includer:

```
class Base
  include Validations
  extend Validations::ClassMethods
  # ...
```

Include-and-extend allows you to skip the extend line and just write the include line. You might argue that removing this line from Base isn't worth the additional complexity in Validations.

However, complexity is not include-and-extend's only shortcoming. The trick also has a deeper issue—one that deserves a close look.

The Problem of Chained Inclusions

Imagine that you include a module that includes another module. You've seen an example of this in *The Validations Modules*: ActiveRecord::Base includes ActiveRecord::Validations, which includes ActiveModel::Validations. What would happen if both modules used the include-and-extend trick? You can find an answer by looking at this minimal example:

part2/chained_inclusions_broken.rb

```
module SecondLevelModule
  def self.included(base)
    base.extend ClassMethods
  end

  def second_level_instance_method; 'ok'; end

  module ClassMethods
    def second_level_class_method; 'ok'; end
  end
end

module FirstLevelModule
  def self.included(base)
    base.extend ClassMethods
  end

  def first_level_instance_method; 'ok'; end

  module ClassMethods
    def first_level_class_method; 'ok'; end
```

```
  end

  include SecondLevelModule
end

class BaseClass
  include FirstLevelModule
end
```

BaseClass includes FirstLevelModule, which in turn includes SecondLevelModule. Both modules get in BaseClass's chain of ancestors, so you can call both modules' instance methods on an instance of BaseClass:

```
BaseClass.new.first_level_instance_method      # => "ok"
BaseClass.new.second_level_instance_method     # => "ok"
```

Thanks to include-and-extend, methods in FirstLevelModule::ClassMethods also become class methods on BaseClass:

```
BaseClass.first_level_class_method                 # => "ok"
```

SecondLevelModule also uses include-and-extend, so you might expect methods in SecondLevelModule::ClassMethods to become class methods on BaseClass. However, the trick doesn't work in this case:

```
BaseClass.second_level_class_method                # => NoMethodError
```

Go through the code step by step, and you'll see where the problem is. When Ruby calls SecondLevelModule.included, the base parameter is not BaseClass, but FirstLevelModule. As a result, the methods in SecondLevelModule::ClassMethods become class methods on FirstLevelModule—which is not what we wanted.

Rails 2 did include a fix to this problem, but the fix wasn't pretty: instead of using include-and-extend in both the FirstLevelModule and the SecondLevelModule, Rails used it only in the FirstLevelModule. Then FirstLevelModule#included forced the includer to also include the SecondLevelModule, like this:

part2/chained_inclusions_fixed.rb

```
module FirstLevelModule
  def self.included(base)
    base.extend ClassMethods
    base.send :include, SecondLevelModule
  end

  # ...
```

Distressingly, the code above made the entire system less flexible; it forced Rails to distinguish first-level modules from other modules, and each module had to know whether it was supposed to be first-level. (To make things clumsier, Rails couldn't call Module#include directly, because it was a private method—so it had to use a *Dynamic Dispatch (48)* instead. Recent rubies made include public, but we're talking ancient history here.)

At this point in our story, you'd be forgiven for thinking that include-and-extend created more problems than it solved in the first place. This trick forced multiple modules to contain the same boilerplate code, and it failed if you had more than one level of module inclusions. To address these issues, the authors of Rails crafted ActiveSupport::Concern.

ActiveSupport::Concern

ActiveSupport::Concern encapsulates the include-and-extend trick and fixes the problem of chained inclusions. A module can get this functionality by extending Concern and defining its own ClassMethods module:

`part2/using_concern.rb`

```ruby
require 'active_support'

module MyConcern
  extend ActiveSupport::Concern

  def an_instance_method; "an instance method"; end

  module ClassMethods
    def a_class_method; "a class method"; end
  end
end

class MyClass
  include MyConcern
end

MyClass.new.an_instance_method  # => "an instance method"
MyClass.a_class_method          # => "a class method"
```

In the rest of this chapter I'll use the word "concern" with a lowercase C to mean "a module that extends ActiveSupport::Concern," like MyConcern does in the example above. In modern Rails, most modules are concerns, including ActiveRecord::Validations and ActiveModel::Validations.

Let's see how Concern works its magic.

A Look at Concern's Source Code

The source code of Concern is quite short but also fairly complicated. It defines just two important methods: extended and append_features. Here is extended:

`gems/activesupport-4.1.0/lib/active_support/concern.rb`

```ruby
module ActiveSupport
  module Concern
```

```ruby
class MultipleIncludedBlocks < StandardError #:nodoc:
  def initialize
    super "Cannot define multiple 'included' blocks for a Concern"
  end
end

def self.extended(base)
  base.instance_variable_set(:@_dependencies, [])
end

# ...
```

When a module extends Concern, Ruby calls the extended *Hook Method (157)*, and extended defines an @_dependencies *Class Instance Variable (110)* on the extender. I'll show you what happens to this variable in a few pages. For now, just remember that all concerns have it, and it's initially an empty array.

To introduce Concern#append_features, the other important method in Concern, let me take you on a very short side-trip into Ruby's standard libraries.

Module#append_features

Module#append_features is a core Ruby method. It's similar to Module#included, in that Ruby will call it whenever you include a module. However, there is an important difference between append_features and included: included is a Hook Method that is normally empty, and it exists only in case you want to override it. By contrast, append_features is where the real inclusion happens. append_features checks whether the included module is already in the includer's chain of ancestors, and if it's not, it adds the module to the chain.

There is a reason why you didn't read about append_features in the first part of this book: in your normal coding, you're supposed to override included, not append_features. If you override append_features, you can get some surprising results, as in the following example:

part2/append_features.rb

```ruby
module M
  def self.append_features(base); end
end

class C
  include M
end

C.ancestors   # => [C, Object, Kernel, BasicObject]
```

As the code above shows, by overriding append_features you can prevent a module from being included at all. Interestingly, that's exactly what Concern wants to do, as we'll see soon.

Concern#append_features

Concern defines its own version of append_features.

gems/activesupport-4.1.0/lib/active_support/concern.rb

```ruby
module ActiveSupport
  module Concern
    def append_features(base)
        # ...
```

Remember the *Class Extension (130)* spell? append_features is an instance method on Concern, so it becomes a class method on modules that extend Concern. For example, if a module named Validations extends Concern, then it gains a Validation.append_features class method. If this sounds confusing, look at this picture showing the relationships between Module, Concern, Validations, and Validations's singleton class:

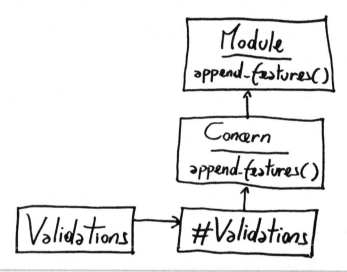

Figure 9—ActiveSupport::Concern overrides Module#append_features.

Let's recap what we've learned so far. First, modules that extend Concern get an @_dependencies Class Variable. Second, they get an override of append_features. With those two concepts in place, we can look at the code that makes Concern tick.

Inside Concern#append_features

Here is the code in Concern#append_features:

gems/activesupport-4.1.0/lib/active_support/concern.rb

```ruby
module ActiveSupport
```

```ruby
module Concern
  def append_features(base)
    if base.instance_variable_defined?(:@_dependencies)
      base.instance_variable_get(:@_dependencies) << self
      return false
    else
      return false if base < self
      @_dependencies.each { |dep| base.send(:include, dep) }
      super
      base.extend const_get(:ClassMethods) \
        if const_defined?(:ClassMethods)
      # ...
    end
  end
end

# ...
```

This is a hard piece of code to wrap your brain around, but its basic idea is simple: never include a concern in another concern. Instead, when concerns try to include each other, just link them in a graph of dependencies. When a concern is finally included by a module that is not itself a concern, roll all of its dependencies into the includer in one fell swoop.

Let's look at the code step by step. To understand it, remember that it is executed as a class method of the concern. In this scope, self is the concern, and base is the module that is including it, which might or might not be a concern itself.

When you enter append_features, you want to check whether your includer is itself a concern. If it has an @_dependencies Class Variable, then you know it is a concern. In this case, instead of adding yourself to your includer's chain of ancestors, you just add yourself to its list of dependencies, and you return false to signal that no inclusion actually happened. For example, this happens if you are ActiveModel::Validations, and you get included by ActiveRecord::Validations.

What happens if your includer is *not* itself a concern—for example, when you are ActiveRecord::Validations, and you get included by ActiveRecord::Base? In this case, you check whether you're already an ancestor of this includer, maybe because you were included via another chain of concerns. (That's the meaning of base < self.) If you are not, you come to the crucial point of the entire exercise: you recursively include your dependencies in your includer. This minimalistic dependency management system solves the issue that you've read about in *The Problem of Chained Inclusions*, on page 181.

After rolling all your dependent concerns into your includer's chain of ancestors, you still have a couple of things to do. First, you must add *yourself* to that chain of ancestors, by calling the standard Module.append_features with super. Finally, don't forget what this entire machinery is for: you have to extend the includer with your own ClassMethods module, like the include-and-extend trick does. You need Kernel#const_get to get a reference to ClassMethods, because you must read the constant from the scope of self, not the scope of the Concern module, where this code is physically located.

Concern also contains some more functionality, but you've seen enough to grasp the idea behind this module.

Concern Wrap-Up

ActiveSupport::Concern is a minimalistic dependency management system, wrapped into a single module with just a few lines of code. That code is complicated, but using Concern is easy, as you can see by looking into Active Model's source:

gems/activemodel-4.1.0/lib/active_model/validations.rb

```
module ActiveModel
  module Validations
    extend ActiveSupport::Concern
    # ...

    module ClassMethods
      def validate(*args, &block)
        # ...
```

Just by doing the above, ActiveModel::Validations adds a validate class method to ActiveRecord::Base, without worrying about the fact that ActiveRecord::Validations happens to be in the middle. Concern will work behind to scenes to sort out the dependencies between concerns.

Is ActiveSupport::Concern too clever for its own good? That's up to you to decide. Some programmers think that Concern hides too much magic behind a seemingly innocuous call to include, and this hidden complexity carries hidden costs.[1] Other programmers praise Concern for helping to keep Rails' modules as slim and simple as they can be.

Whatever your take on ActiveSupport::Concern, you can learn a lot by exploring its insides. Here is one lesson I personally took away from this exploration.

A Lesson Learned

In most languages, there aren't many ways to bind components together. Maybe you inherit from a class or you delegate to an object. If you want to

---

1. http://blog.coreyhaines.com/2012/12/why-i-dont-use-activesupportconcern.html

get fancy, then you can use a library that specializes in managing dependencies—or even an entire framework.

Now, see how the authors of Rails bound their framework's parts together. In the very beginning, they probably just included and extended modules. Later, they sprinkled their code with metaprogramming fairy dust, introducing the include-and-extend idiom. Still later, as Rails kept growing, that idiom started creaking around the edges—so they replaced include-and-extend with the metaprogramming-heavy ActiveSupport::Concern. They evolved their own dependencies management system, one step at a time.

Over the years, we've learned that software design is not a "get it right the first time" affair. This is especially true in a malleable language such as Ruby, where you can use metaprogramming to change something as fundamental as the way that modules interact. So here is the main lesson I gained from the story of Concern: *metaprogramming is not about being clever—it's about being flexible.*

When I write my code, I don't strive for a perfect design at the beginning, and I don't use complex metaprogramming spells before I need them. Instead, I try to keep my code simple, using the most obvious techniques that do the job. Maybe at some point my code gets tangled, or I spot some stubborn duplication. That's when I reach for sharper tools, such as metaprogramming.

This book is full of metaprogramming success stories, and ActiveSupport::Concern is yet another one of them. However, Concern's complex code and mildly controversial nature hint at a darker side of metaprogramming. This will be the subject of the next chapter, where we'll look at the story of Rails' most infamous methods.

The Rise and Fall of alias_method_chain

In the previous two chapters, we looked at the modular design of Rails and how that design changed over time. Now I'll tell you of a more dramatic change in Rails' history: how a method named alias_method_chain rose to fame, fell in disgrace, and was eventually scrapped almost entirely from the Rails codebase.

The Rise of alias_method_chain

In *The Include-and-Extend Trick*, on page 179, I showed you a snippet of code from an old version of Rails...minus a few interesting lines. Here is the same code again, with those lines now visible and marked with arrows:

gems/activerecord-2.3.2/lib/active_record/validations.rb

```
module ActiveRecord
  module Validations

    def self.included(base)
      base.extend ClassMethods
➤     base.class_eval do
➤       alias_method_chain :save, :validation
➤       alias_method_chain :save!, :validation
➤     end

      # ...

    end
```

When ActiveRecord::Base includes the Validations module, the marked lines reopen Base and call a method named alias_method_chain. Let me show you a quick example to explain what alias_method_chain does.

The Reason for alias_method_chain

Suppose you have a module that defines a greet method. It might look like the following code.

```
part2/greet_with_aliases.rb
module Greetings
  def greet
    "hello"
  end
end

class MyClass
  include Greetings
end

MyClass.new.greet  # => "hello"
```

Now suppose you want to wrap optional functionality around greet—for example, you want your greetings to be a bit more enthusiastic. You can do that with a couple of *Around Aliases (134)*:

```
class MyClass
  include Greetings

  def greet_with_enthusiasm
    "Hey, #{greet_without_enthusiasm}!"
  end

  alias_method :greet_without_enthusiasm, :greet
  alias_method :greet, :greet_with_enthusiasm
end

MyClass.new.greet  # => "Hey, hello!"
```

I defined two new methods: greet_without_enthusiasm and greet_with_enthusiasm. The first method is just an alias of the original greet. The second method calls the first method and also wraps some happiness around it. I also aliased greet to the new enthusiastic method—so the callers of greet will get the enthusiastic behavior by default, unless they explicitly avoid it by calling greet_without_enthusiasm instead:

```
MyClass.new.greet_without_enthusiasm  # => "hello"
```

To sum it all up, the original greet is now called greet_without_enthusiasm. If you want the enthusiastic behavior, you can call either greet_with_enthusiasm or greet, which are actually aliases of the same method.

This idea of wrapping a new feature around an existing method is common in Rails. In all cases, you end up with three methods that follow the naming conventions I just showed you: method, method_with_feature, and method_without_feature. The first two methods include the new feature. The third doesn't.

Instead of duplicating these aliases all over the place, Rails provided a metaprogramming method that did it all for you. It was named Module#alias_method_chain, and it was part of the Active Support library. I'm saying "it was" rather than "it is" for reasons that will be clear soon—but if you look inside Active Support, you'll find alias_method_chain is still there. Let's look at it.

Inside alias_method_chain

Here is the code of alias_method_chain:

gems/activesupport-4.1.0/lib/active_support/core_ext/module/aliasing.rb

```ruby
class Module
  def alias_method_chain(target, feature)
    # Strip out punctuation on predicates or bang methods since
    # e.g. target?_without_feature is not a valid method name.
    aliased_target, punctuation = target.to_s.sub(/([?!=])$/, ''), $1
    yield(aliased_target, punctuation) if block_given?

    with_method = "#{aliased_target}_with_#{feature}#{punctuation}"
    without_method = "#{aliased_target}_without_#{feature}#{punctuation}"

    alias_method without_method, target
    alias_method target, with_method

    case
    when public_method_defined?(without_method)
      public target
    when protected_method_defined?(without_method)
      protected target
    when private_method_defined?(without_method)
      private target
    end
  end
end
```

alias_method_chain takes the name of a target method and the name of an additional feature. From those two, it calculates the name of two new methods: target_without_feature and target_with_feature. Then it stores away the original target as target_without_feature, and it aliases target_with_feature to target (assuming that a method called target_with_feature is defined somewhere in the same module). Finally, the case switch sets the visibility of target_without_feature so that it's the same visibility as the original target.

alias_method_chain also has a few more features, such as yielding to a block so that the caller can override the default naming, and dealing with methods that end with an exclamation or a question mark—but essentially, it just builds an *Around Alias (134)*. Let's see how this mechanism was used in ActiveRecord::Validations.

One Last Look at Validations

Here is the code from the old version of ActiveRecord::Validations again:

```
def self.included(base)
  base.extend ClassMethods
  # ...
  base.class_eval do
    alias_method_chain :save, :validation
    alias_method_chain :save!, :validation
  end
  # ...
end
```

These lines reopen the ActiveRecord::Base class and hack its save and save! methods to add validation. This aliasing ensures that you will get automatic validation whenever you save an object to the database. If you want to save without validating, you can call the aliased versions of the original method, now called save_without_validation.

For the entire scheme to work, the Validations module still needs to define two methods named save_with_validation and save_with_validation!:

gems/activerecord-2.3.2/lib/active_record/validations.rb

```
module ActiveRecord
  module Validations
    def save_with_validation(perform_validation = true)
      if perform_validation && valid? || !perform_validation
        save_without_validation
      else
        false
      end
    end
    def save_with_validation!
      if valid?
        save_without_validation!
      else
        raise RecordInvalid.new(self)
      end
    end
    def valid?
      # ...
```

The actual validation happens in the valid? method. Validation#save_with_validation returns false if the validation fails, unless the caller explicitly disables validation. Otherwise, it just calls the original save_without_validation. Validation#save_with_validation! raises an exception if the validation fails, and otherwise falls back to the original save_without_validation!.

This is how alias_method_chain was used around the times of Rails 2. Things have changed since then, as I will explain next.

The Fall of alias_method_chain

In the previous two chapters, you've seen that the libraries in Rails are mostly built by assembling modules. Back in Rails 2, many of those modules used alias_method_chain to wrap functionality around the methods of their includers. The authors of libraries that extended Rails adopted the same mechanism to wrap their own functionality around the Rails methods. As a result, alias_method_chain was used all over the place, both in Rails and in dozens of third-party libraries.

alias_method_chain was good at removing duplicated aliases, but it also came with a few problems of its own. For a start, alias_method_chain is just an encapsulation of an *Around Alias (134)*, and Around Aliases have the subtle problems that you might remember from *The Thor Example*, on page 133. To make things worse, alias_method_chain turned out to be too clever for its own good: with all the method renaming and shuffling that was going on in Rails, it could become hard to track which version of a method you were actually calling.

However, the most damning issue of alias_method_chain was that it was simply unnecessary in most cases. Ruby is an object-oriented language, so it provides a more elegant, built-in way of wrapping functionality around an existing method. Think back to our example of adding enthusiasm to the greet method:

`part2/greet_with_super.rb`

```ruby
module Greetings
  def greet
    "hello"
  end
end

class MyClass
  include Greetings
end

MyClass.new.greet  # => "hello"
```

Instead of using aliases to wrap additional functionality around greet, you can just redefine greet in a separate module and include that module instead:

`part2/greet_with_super.rb`

```ruby
module EnthusiasticGreetings
```

```ruby
  include Greetings

  def greet
    "Hey, #{super}!"
  end
end

class MyClass
  include EnthusiasticGreetings
end

MyClass.ancestors[0..2]  # => [MyClass, EnthusiasticGreetings, Greetings]
MyClass.new.greet        # => "Hey, hello!"
```

The chain of ancestors of MyClass includes EnthusiasticGreetings and then Greetings, in that order. That's why by calling greet, you end up calling EnthusiasticGreetings#greet, and EnthusiasticGreetings#greet can in turn call into Greetings#greet with super. This solution is not as glamorous as alias_method_chain, but it's simpler and all the better for it. Recent versions of ActiveRecord::Validations acknowledge that simplicity by using a regular override instead of alias_method_chain:

gems/activerecord-4.1.0/lib/active_record/validations.rb

```ruby
module ActiveRecord
  module Validations
    # The validation process on save can be skipped by passing
    # <tt>validate: false</tt>.
    # The regular Base#save method is replaced with this when the
    # validations module is mixed in, which it is by default.
    def save(options={})
      perform_validations(options) ? super : false
    end

    # Attempts to save the record just like Base#save but will raise
    # a +RecordInvalid+ exception instead of returning +false+ if
    # the record is not valid.
    def save!(options={})
      perform_validations(options) ? super : raise(RecordInvalid.new(self))
    end

    def perform_validations(options={})
      # ...
```

Validation#save performs the actual validation (by calling the private method perform_validations). If the validation succeeds, then it proceeds with the normal save code in ActiveRecord::Base by calling super. If the validation fails, then it returns false. Validation#save! follows the same steps, except that it raises an exception if the validation fails.

These days, Rails barely ever uses alias_method_chain. You can still find this method called inside Active Support and some third-party libraries, but there is no trace of it in libraries such as Active Record. The once-popular alias_method_chain has nearly disappeared from the Rails environment.

However, there is still one case where you might argue that alias_method_chain works better than its object-oriented alternative. Let's look at it.

The Birth of Module#prepend

Let's add a twist to our ongoing greet method example: instead of defining greet in a module, let's assume it's defined directly in the class.

`part2/greet_with_prepend.rb`

```ruby
class MyClass
  def greet
    "hello"
  end
end

MyClass.new.greet  # => "hello"
```

In this case, you cannot wrap functionality around greet by simply including a module that overrides it:

`part2/greet_with_prepend_broken.rb`

```ruby
module EnthusiasticGreetings
  def greet
    "Hey, #{super}!"
  end
end

class MyClass
  include EnthusiasticGreetings
end

MyClass.ancestors[0..2]  # => [MyClass, EnthusiasticGreetings, Object]
MyClass.new.greet        # => "hello"
```

The code above shows that when you include EnthusiasticGreetings, that module gets higher than the class in the class's chain of ancestors. As a result, the greet method in the class overrides the greet method in the module, instead of the other way around.

You could solve this problem by extracting greet from MyClass into its own module, like the Greetings module in the previous section. If you do that, you'll be able to insert an intermediary module like EnthusiasticGreetings in the chain and use the override-and-call-super technique, just as we did back then. However, you might be unable to do that—for example, because MyClass is part of a library such as Rails, and you're extending that library rather than working directly on its source code. This limitation is the main reason why many Rubyists still use alias_method_chain when they extend Rails.

However, Ruby 2.0 came with an elegant solution for this problem in the form of Module#prepend:

```ruby
module EnthusiasticGreetings
  def greet
    "Hey, #{super}!"
  end
end

class MyClass
  prepend EnthusiasticGreetings
end

MyClass.ancestors[0..2]   # => [EnthusiasticGreetings, MyClass, Object]
MyClass.new.greet         # => "Hey, hello!"
```

This is a *Prepended Wrapper (136)*, a modern alternative to *Around Aliases (134)*. Because we used prepend, the EnthusiasticGreetings#greet got lower than MyClass#greet in MyClass's chain of ancestors, so we went back to the usual trick of overriding greet and calling super.

As I write, Rails is not using Module#prepend yet, because it's still aiming to be compatible with Ruby 1.9. When Rails eventually drops this constraint, I expect that prepend will make its appearance in Rails and its extensions. At that point, there will be no urgent reason to call alias_method_chain anymore.

A Lesson Learned

Throughout this book I showed you how convenient, elegant, and cool metaprogramming can be. The story of alias_method_chain, however, is a cautionary tale: metaprogramming code can sometimes get complicated, and it can even cause you to overlook more traditional, simpler techniques. In particular, sometimes you can avoid metaprogramming and use plain, old-fashioned object-oriented programming instead.

The lesson I personally learned from this story is: *resist the temptation to be too clever in your code*. Ask yourself whether there is a simpler way to reach your goal than metaprogramming. If the answer is no, then go forth and metaprogram the heck out of your problem. In many cases, however, you'll find that a more straightforward OOP approach does the job just as well.

In this chapter, I showed you that metaprogramming can be overused and sometimes replaced with simpler techniques. To be fair, however, metaprogramming is still one of the tastier ingredients in the Rails pie. In the next chapter, I'll show you how one of Rails' defining features owes its very existence to a clever mix of metaprogramming tricks.

The Evolution of Attribute Methods

By this point in your reading, you've seen plenty of metaprogramming snippets and examples. However, you might still wonder what happens when you use metaprogramming in a real, large system. How do these sophisticated techniques fare in the messy world out there, where code often grows in complexity and evolves in unexpected directions?

To answer this question, we will close our tour with a look at attribute methods, one of Rails' most popular features. Their source code contains a lot of metaprogramming, and it has been changing constantly since the first version of Rails. If we track the history of attribute methods, we'll see what happened as their code became more complicated and nuanced.

One word of warning before we begin: there is plenty of complex code in this chapter, and it would be pointless to explain it in too much detail. Instead, I'll just try to make a point by giving you a high-level idea of what's going on. Don't feel as if you have to understand each and every line of code as you read through the next few pages.

Let's start with a quick example of attribute methods.

Attribute Methods in Action

Assume that you've created a database table that contains tasks.

```
part2/ar_attribute_methods.rb
require 'active_record'
ActiveRecord::Base.establish_connection :adapter => "sqlite3",
                                        :database => "dbfile"

ActiveRecord::Base.connection.create_table :tasks do |t|
  t.string   :description
  t.boolean  :completed
end
```

Now you can define an empty Task class that inherits from ActiveRecord::Base, and you can use objects of that class to interact with the database:

```
class Task < ActiveRecord::Base; end

task = Task.new
task.description = 'Clean up garage'
task.completed = true
task.save

task.description    # => "Clean up garage"
task.completed?     # => true
```

The previous code calls four accessor methods to read and write the object's attributes: two write accessors (description= and completed=), one read accessor (description), and one query accessor (completed?). None of these *Mimic Methods (218)* comes from the definition of Task. Instead, Active Record generated them by looking at the columns of the tasks table. These automatically generated accessors are called *attribute methods*.

You probably expect that attribute methods such as description= are either *Ghost Methods (57)* implemented through method_missing or *Dynamic Methods (51)* defined with define_method. Things are actually more complicated than that, as you'll find out soon.

A History of Complexity

Instead of looking at the current implementation of attribute methods, let me go all the way back to 2004—the year that Rails 1.0.0 was unleashed on an unsuspecting world.

Rails 1: Simple Beginnings

In the very first version of Rails, the implementation of attribute methods was just a few lines of code:

gems/activerecord-1.0.0/lib/active_record/base.rb

```
module ActiveRecord
  class Base
    def initialize(attributes = nil)
      @attributes = attributes_from_column_definition
      # ...
    end

    def attribute_names
      @attributes.keys.sort
    end

    alias_method :respond_to_without_attributes?, :respond_to?
```

```
def respond_to?(method)
  @@dynamic_methods ||= attribute_names +
                        attribute_names.collect { |attr| attr + "=" } +
                        attribute_names.collect { |attr| attr + "?" }
  @@dynamic_methods.include?(method.to_s) ?
                                      true :
                                      respond_to_without_attributes?(method)
end

def method_missing(method_id, *arguments)
  method_name = method_id.id2name

  if method_name =~ read_method? && @attributes.include?($1)
    return read_attribute($1)
  elsif method_name =~ write_method?
    write_attribute($1, arguments[0])
  elsif method_name =~ query_method?
    return query_attribute($1)
  else
    super
  end
end

def read_method?()  /^([a-zA-Z][-_\w]*)[^=?]*$/ end
def write_method?() /^([a-zA-Z][-_\w]*)=.*$/    end
def query_method?() /^([a-zA-Z][-_\w]*)\?$/     end

def read_attribute(attr_name)         # ...
def write_attribute(attr_name, value) #...
def query_attribute(attr_name)        # ...
```

Take a look at the initialize method: when you create an ActiveRecord::Base object, its @attributes instance variable is populated with the name of the attributes from the database. For example, if the relevant table in the database has a column named description, then @attributes will contain the string "description", among others.

Now skip down to method_missing, where those attribute names become the names of *Ghost Methods (57)*. When you call a method such as description=, method_missing notices two things: first, description is the name of an attribute; and second, the name of description= matches the regular expression for write accessors. As a result, method_missing calls write_attribute("description"), which writes the value of the description in the database. A similar process happens for query accessors (that end in a question mark) and read accessors (that are just the same as attribute names).

In Chapter 3, *Tuesday: Methods*, on page 45, you also learned that it's generally a good idea to redefine respond_to? (or respond_to_missing?) together with method_missing. For example, if I can call my_task.description, then I expect that my_task.respond_to?(:description) returns true. The ActiveRecord::Base#respond_to? method is an *Around Alias (134)* of the original respond_to?, and it also checks whether a method name matches the rules for attribute readers, writers, or queries. The overridden respond_to? uses a *Nil Guard (219)* to calculate those names only once, and store them in an @@dynamic_methods class variable.

I stopped short of showing you the code that accesses the database, such as read_attribute, write_attribute, and query_attribute. Apart from that, you've just looked at the entire implementation of attribute methods in Rails 1. By the time Rails 2 came out, however, this code had become more complex.

Rails 2: Focus on Performance

Do you remember the explanation of method_missing in Chapter 3, *Tuesday: Methods*, on page 45? When you call a method that doesn't exist, Ruby walks up the chain of ancestors looking for the method. If it reaches BasicObject without finding the method, then it starts back at the bottom and calls method_missing. This means that, in general, calling a *Ghost Method (57)* is slower than calling a normal method, because Ruby has to walk up the entire chain of ancestors at least once.

In most concrete cases, this difference in performance between Ghost Methods and regular methods is negligible. In Rails, however, attribute methods are called very frequently. In Rails 1, each of those calls also had to walk up ActiveRecord::Base's extremely long chain of ancestors. As a result, performance suffered.

The authors of Rails could solve this performance problem by replacing Ghost Methods with *Dynamic Methods (51)*—using define_method to create read, write, and query accessors for all attributes, and getting rid of method_missing altogether. Interestingly, however, they went for a mixed solution, including *both* Ghost Methods and Dynamic Methods. Let's look at the result.

Ghosts Incarnated

If you check the source code of Rails 2, you'll see that the code for attribute methods moved from ActiveRecord::Base itself to a separate ActiveRecord::AttributeMethods module, which is then included by Base. The original method_missing has also become complicated, so we will discuss it in two separate parts. Here is the first part:

gems/activerecord-2.3.2/lib/active_record/attribute_methods.rb

```ruby
module ActiveRecord
  module AttributeMethods
    def method_missing(method_id, *args, &block)
```

```
  method_name = method_id.to_s

  if self.class.private_method_defined?(method_name)
    raise NoMethodError.new("Attempt to call private method", method_name, args)
  end

  # If we haven't generated any methods yet, generate them, then
  # see if we've created the method we're looking for.
  if !self.class.generated_methods?
    self.class.define_attribute_methods
    if self.class.generated_methods.include?(method_name)
      return self.send(method_id, *args, &block)
    end
  end

  # ...
end

def read_attribute(attr_name)          # ...
def write_attribute(attr_name, value)  # ...
def query_attribute(attr_name)         # ...
```

When you call a method such as Task#description= for the first time, the call is delivered to method_missing. Before it does its job, method_missing ensures that you're not inadvertently bypassing encapsulation and calling a private method. Then it calls an intriguing-sounding define_attribute_methods method.

We'll look at define_attribute_methods in a minute. For now, all you need to know is that it defines read, write, and query *Dynamic Methods (51)* for all the columns in the database. The next time you call description= or any other accessor that maps to a database column, your call isn't handled by method_missing. Instead, you call a real, non-ghost method.

When you entered method_missing, description= was a *Ghost Method (57)*. Now description= is a regular flesh-and-blood method, and method_missing can call it with a *Dynamic Dispatch (48)* and return the result. This process takes place only once for each class that inherits from ActiveRecord::Base. If you enter method_missing a second time for any reason, the class method generated_methods? returns true, and this code is skipped.

The following code shows how define_attribute_methods defines non-ghostly accessors.

gems/activerecord-2.3.2/lib/active_record/attribute_methods.rb

```ruby
# Generates all the attribute related methods for columns in the database
# accessors, mutators and query methods.
def define_attribute_methods
  return if generated_methods?
  columns_hash.each do |name, column|
    unless instance_method_already_implemented?(name)
      if self.serialized_attributes[name]
        define_read_method_for_serialized_attribute(name)
      elsif create_time_zone_conversion_attribute?(name, column)
        define_read_method_for_time_zone_conversion(name)
      else
        define_read_method(name.to_sym, name, column)
      end
    end

    unless instance_method_already_implemented?("#{name}=")
      if create_time_zone_conversion_attribute?(name, column)
        define_write_method_for_time_zone_conversion(name)
      else
        define_write_method(name.to_sym)
      end
    end

    unless instance_method_already_implemented?("#{name}?")
      define_question_method(name)
    end
  end
end
```

The instance_method_already_implemented? method is there to prevent involuntary *Monkeypatches (16)*: if a method by the name of the attribute already exists, then this code skips to the next attribute. Apart from that, the previous code does little but delegate to other methods that do the real work, such as define_read_method or define_write_method.

As an example, take a look at define_write_method. I've marked the most important lines with arrows:

gems/activerecord-2.3.2/lib/active_record/attribute_methods.rb

```ruby
➤  def define_write_method(attr_name)
➤    evaluate_attribute_method attr_name,
➤      "def #{attr_name}=(new_value);write_attribute('#{attr_name}', new_value);end",
➤      "#{attr_name}="
➤  end

➤  def evaluate_attribute_method(attr_name, method_definition, method_name=attr_name)
     unless method_name.to_s == primary_key.to_s
       generated_methods << method_name
     end
```

```
  begin
➤   class_eval(method_definition, __FILE__, __LINE__)
  rescue SyntaxError => err
    generated_methods.delete(attr_name)
    if logger
      logger.warn "Exception occurred during reader method compilation."
      logger.warn "Maybe #{attr_name} is not a valid Ruby identifier?"
      logger.warn err.message
    end
  end
end
```

The define_write_method method builds a *String of Code (141)* that is evaluated by class_eval. For example, if you call description=, then evaluate_attribute_method evaluates this String of Code:

```
def description=(new_value);write_attribute('description', new_value);end
```

Thus the description= method is born. A similar process happens for description, description?, and the accessors for all the other database columns.

Here's a recap of what we've covered so far. When you access an attribute for the first time, that attribute is a *Ghost Method (57)*. ActiveRecord::Base#method_missing takes this chance to turn the Ghost Method into a real method. While it's there, method_missing also dynamically defines read, write, and query accessors for all the other database columns. The next time you call that attribute or another database-backed attribute, you find a real accessor method waiting for you, and you don't have to enter method_missing anymore.

However, this logic doesn't apply to each and every attribute accessor, as you'll discover by looking at the second half of method_missing.

Attributes That Stay Dynamic

As it turns out, there are cases where Active Record doesn't want to define attribute accessors. For example, think of attributes that are not backed by a database column, such as calculated fields:

part2/ar_attribute_methods.rb

```
my_query = "tasks.*, (description like '%garage%') as heavy_job"
task = Task.find(:first, :select => my_query)
task.heavy_job?  # => true
```

Attributes like heavy_job can be different for each object, so there's no point in generating *Dynamic Methods (51)* to access them. The second half of method_missing deals with these attributes:

gems/activerecord-2.3.2/lib/active_record/attribute_methods.rb

```ruby
module ActiveRecord
  module AttributeMethods
    def method_missing(method_id, *args, &block)
      # ...

      if self.class.primary_key.to_s == method_name
        id
      elsif md = self.class.match_attribute_method?(method_name)
        attribute_name, method_type = md.pre_match, md.to_s
        if @attributes.include?(attribute_name)
          __send__("attribute#{method_type}", attribute_name, *args, &block)
        else
          super
        end
      elsif @attributes.include?(method_name)
        read_attribute(method_name)
      else
        super
      end
    end

    private
      # Handle *? for method_missing.
      def attribute?(attribute_name)
        query_attribute(attribute_name)
      end

      # Handle *= for method_missing.
      def attribute=(attribute_name, value)
        write_attribute(attribute_name, value)
      end
```

Look at the code in method_missing above. If you're accessing the object's identifier, then it returns its value. If you're calling an attribute accessor, then it
calls the accessor with either a *Dynamic Dispatch (48)* (for write or query
accessors) or a direct call to read_attribute (for read accessors). Otherwise,
method_missing sends the call up the chain of ancestors with super.

I don't want to waste your time with unnecessary details, so I only showed
you part of the code for attribute methods in Rails 2. What you've seen,
however, shows that both the feature and its code became more complicated
in the second major version of Rails. Let's see how this trend continued in
the following versions.

Rails 3 and 4: More Special Cases

In Rails 1, attribute methods were implemented with a few dozen lines of code. In Rails 2, they had their own file and hundreds of lines of code. In Rails 3, they spanned nine files of source code, not including tests.

As Rails applications became larger and more sophisticated, the authors of the framework kept uncovering small twists, performance optimizations, and corner cases related to attribute methods. The code and the number of metaprogramming tricks it used grew with the number of corner cases. I'll show you only one of those corner cases, but even this single example is too long to fit in this chapter, so I will just show you a few snippets of code as quickly as I can. Brace yourself.

The example I picked is one of the most extreme optimizations in modern Rails. We've seen that Rails 2 improved performance by turning *Ghost Methods (57)* into *Dynamic Methods (51)*. Rails 4 goes one step further: when it defines an attribute accessor, it also turns it into an UnboundMethod and stores it in a method cache. If a second class has an attribute by the same name, and hence needs the same accessor, Rails 4 just retrieves the previously defined accessor from the cache and binds it to the second class. This way, if different attributes in separate classes happen to have the same name, then Rails defines only a single set of accessor methods and reuses those methods for all attributes. (I'm as surprised as you are that this optimization has a visible effect on performance—but in the case of Rails, it does.)

I'll start with code from deep inside the attribute methods implementation:

gems/activerecord-4.1.0/lib/active_record/attribute_methods/read.rb

```
module ActiveRecord
  module AttributeMethods
    module Read
      extend ActiveSupport::Concern

      module ClassMethods
        if Module.methods_transplantable?
          def define_method_attribute(name)
            method = ReaderMethodCache[name]
            generated_attribute_methods.module_eval { define_method name, method }
          end
        else
          def define_method_attribute(name)
            # ...
          end
        end
      end
```

This code defines a method named define_method_attribute. This method will ultimately become a class method of ActiveRecord::Base, thanks to the mechanism we discussed in Chapter 10, *Active Support's Concern Module*, on page 179. Here, however, comes a twist: define_method_attribute is defined differently depending on the result of the Module.methods_transplantable? method.

Module.methods_transplantable? comes from the Active Support library, and it answers one very specific question: can I bind an UnboundMethod to an object of a different class? In *Unbound Methods*, on page 94, I mentioned that you can only do that from Ruby 2.0 onward, so this code defines define_method_attribute in two different ways depending on whether you're running Rails on Ruby 1.9 or 2.x.

Assume that you're running Ruby 2.0 or later. In this case, define_method_attribute retrieves an UnboundMethod from a cache of methods, and it binds the method to the current module with define_method. The cache of methods is stored in a constant named ReaderMethodCache.

(The call to generated_attribute_methods might look confusing—it returns a *Clean Room (87)* that serializes method definitions happening in different threads.)

Let's go see how ReaderMethodCache is initialized. The long comment gives an idea of how tricky it must have been to write this code:

gems/activerecord-4.1.0/lib/active_record/attribute_methods/read.rb

```
module ActiveRecord
  module AttributeMethods
    module Read
      ReaderMethodCache = Class.new(AttributeMethodCache) {
        private
        # We want to generate the methods via module_eval rather than
        # define_method, because define_method is slower on dispatch.
        # Evaluating many similar methods may use more memory as the instruction
        # sequences are duplicated and cached (in MRI).  define_method may
        # be slower on dispatch, but if you're careful about the closure
        # created, then define_method will consume much less memory.
        #
        # But sometimes the database might return columns with
        # characters that are not allowed in normal method names (like
        # 'my_column(omg)'. So to work around this we first define with
        # the __temp__ identifier, and then use alias method to rename
        # it to what we want.
        #
        # We are also defining a constant to hold the frozen string of
        # the attribute name. Using a constant means that we do not have
        # to allocate an object on each call to the attribute method.
        # Making it frozen means that it doesn't get duped when used to
```

```
      # key the @attributes_cache in read_attribute.
      def method_body(method_name, const_name)
        <<-EOMETHOD
        def #{method_name}
          name = ::ActiveRecord::AttributeMethods::AttrNames::ATTR_#{const_name}
          read_attribute(name) { |n| missing_attribute(n, caller) }
        end
        EOMETHOD
      end
    }.new
```

ReaderMethodCache is an instance of an anonymous class—a subclass of AttributeMethodCache. This class defines a single method that returns a *String of Code (141)*. (If you're perplexed by the call to Class.new, take a look back at *Quiz: Class Taboo*, on page 112. If you don't understand the EOMETHOD lines, read about "here documents" in *The REST Client Example*, on page 141.)

Let's leave ReaderMethodCache for a moment and move to the definition of its superclass AttributeMethodCache:

gems/activerecord-4.1.0/lib/active_record/attribute_methods.rb

```
module ActiveRecord
  module AttributeMethods
    AttrNames = Module.new {
      def self.set_name_cache(name, value)
        const_name = "ATTR_#{name}"
        unless const_defined? const_name
          const_set const_name, value.dup.freeze
        end
      end
    }

    class AttributeMethodCache
      def initialize
        @module = Module.new
        @method_cache = ThreadSafe::Cache.new
      end
      def [](name)
        @method_cache.compute_if_absent(name) do
          safe_name = name.unpack('h*').first
          temp_method = "__temp__#{safe_name}"
          ActiveRecord::AttributeMethods::AttrNames.set_name_cache safe_name, name
          @module.module_eval method_body(temp_method, safe_name),
                          __FILE__, __LINE__
          @module.instance_method temp_method
        end
      end

      private
      def method_body; raise NotImplementedError; end
```

end

First, look at AttrNames: it's a module with one single method, set_name_cache. Given a name and a value, set_name_cache defines a conventionally named constant with that value. For example, if you pass it the string "description", then it defines a constant named ATTR_description. AttrNames is somewhat similar to a *Clean Room (87)*; it only exists to store constants that represent the names of attributes.

Now move down to AttributeMethodCache. Its [] method takes the name of an attribute, and it returns an accessor to that attribute as an UnboundMethod. It also takes care of at least one important special case: attribute accessors are Ruby methods, but not all attributes names are valid Ruby method names. (You can read one counterexample in the comment to ReaderMethod-Cache#method_body above.) This code solves that problem by decoding the attribute name to an hexadecimal sequence and creating a conventional safe method name from it.

Once it has a safe name for the accessor, AttributeMethodCache#[] calls method_body to get a String of Code that defines the accessor's body, and it defines the accessor inside a Clean Room named simply @module. (We discussed additional arguments to the *eval methods, such as _FILE_ and _LINE_, in *The irb Example*, on page 144.) Finally, AttributeMethodCache#[] gets the newly created accessor method from the Clean Room and returns it as an UnboundMethod.

On subsequent calls, AttributeMethodCache#[] won't need to define the method anymore. Instead, @method_cache.compute_if_absent will store the result and return it automatically. This policy shaves some time off in cases where the same accessor is defined on multiple classes.

To close the loop, look back at the code of ReaderMethodCache. By overriding method_body and returning the String of Code for a read accessor, ReaderMethod-Cache turns the generic AttributeMethodCache into a cache for read accessors. As you might expect, there is also a WriterMethodCache class that takes care of write accessors.

Is your head spinning a little after this long explanation? Mine is. This example shows how deep and complex attribute methods have become, how many special cases they have covered, and how much they've changed since their simple beginnings. Now we can draw some general conclusions.

A Lesson Learned

Here is one question that developers often ask themselves: How many special cases should I cover in my code? On one extreme, you could always strive for code that is perfect right from the start and leaves no stones unturned. Let's call this approach *Do It Right the First Time*. On the other extreme, you might put together some simple code that just solves your obvious problem today, and maybe make it more comprehensive later, as you uncover more special cases. Let's call this approach *Evolutionary Design*. The act of designing code largely consists of striking the right balance between these two approaches.

What do Rails' attribute methods teach us about design? In Rails 1, the code for accessor methods was so simple, you might consider it simplistic. While it was correct and good enough for simple cases, it ignored many nonobvious use cases, and its performance turned out to be problematic in large applications. As the needs of Rails users evolved, the authors of the framework kept working to make it more flexible. This is a great example of Evolutionary Design.

Think back to the optimization in *Rails 2: Focus on Performance*, on page 202. Most attribute accessors, in particular those that are backed by database tables, start their lives as *Ghost Methods (57)*. When you access an attribute for the first time, Active Record takes the opportunity to turn most of those ghosts into *Dynamic Methods (51)*. Some other accessors, such as accessors to calculated fields, never become real methods, and they remain ghosts forever.

This is one of a number of different possible designs. The authors of Active Record had no shortage of alternatives, including the following:

- Never define accessors dynamically, relying on Ghost Methods exclusively.

- Define accessors when you create the object, in the initialize method.

- Define accessors only for the attribute that is being accessed, not for the other attributes.

- Always define all accessors for each object, including accessors for calculated fields.

- Define accessors with define_method instead of a String of Code.

I don't know about you, but I wouldn't have been able to pick among all of these options just by guessing which ones are faster. How did the authors of Active Record settle on the current design? You can easily imagine them trying a few alternative designs, then profiling their code in a real-life system to discover where the performance bottlenecks were...and *then* optimizing.

The previous example focused on optimizations, but the same principles apply to all aspects of Rails' design. Think about the code in Rails 2 that prevents you from using method_missing to call a private method—or the code in Rails 4 that maps column names in the database to safe Ruby method names. You could certainly foresee special cases such as these, but catching them all could prove very hard. It's arguably easier to cover a reasonable number of special cases like Rails 1 did, and then change your code as more special cases become visible.

Rails' approach seems to be very much biased toward Evolutionary Design rather than Do It Right the First Time. There are two obvious reasons for that. First, Ruby is a flexible, pliable language, especially when you use metaprogramming, so it's generally easy to evolve your code as you go. And second, writing perfect metaprogramming code up front can be hard, because it can be difficult to uncover every possible corner case.

To sum it all up in a single sentence: *keep your code as simple as possible, and add complexity as you need it.* When you start, strive to make your code correct in the general cases, and simple enough that you can add more special cases later. This is a good rule of thumb for most code, but it seems to be especially relevant when metaprogramming is involved.

This last consideration also leads us to a final, deeper lesson—one that has to do with the meaning of metaprogramming itself.

One Final Lesson

We've been together on a daring adventure, starting with the very basics of metaprogramming and closing with a tour of the Rails source code. Before we part, there is one last insight that I will share—possibly the most important of them all.

Metaprogramming Is Just Programming

When I started learning metaprogramming, it looked like magic. I felt like leaving my usual programming behind to enter a new world—a world that was surprising, exciting, and sometimes a bit scary.

As I finish revising this book, the feeling of magic is still there. However, I realize now that in practice there is no hard line separating metaprogramming from plain old vanilla programming. Metaprogramming is just another powerful set of coding tools that you can wield to write code that's simple, clean, and well tested.

I'll go out on a limb to make a bolder assertion: with Ruby, the distinction between metaprogramming and regular code is fuzzy—and ultimately pointless. Once you have an in-depth understanding of the language, you'll have a hard time deciding which techniques and idioms are "meta" and which ones are plain old programming.

In fact, metaprogramming is so deeply ingrained in Ruby that you can barely write an idiomatic Ruby program without using a few metaprogramming spells. The language actually *expects* that you'll tweak the object model, reopen classes, define methods dynamically, and manage scopes with blocks. As Bill might say in a Zen moment, "There is no such thing as metaprogramming. It's just programming all the way down."

Part III

Appendixes

Common Idioms

This appendix is a mixed bag of popular Ruby idioms. They aren't really "meta," so they don't fit into the main story of this book. However, they're so common and they're the foundation of so many metaprogramming spells that you'll probably want to get familiar with them.

Mimic Methods

Much of Ruby's appeal comes from its flexible syntax. You can find an example of this flexiblity even in the most basic program:

```
puts 'Hello, world'
```

Newcomers to Ruby often mistake puts for a language keyword, when it's actually a method. People usually leave out the parentheses when calling puts, so it doesn't look like a method. Reinsert the parentheses, and the nature of puts becomes obvious:

```
puts('Hello, world')
```

Thanks to disguised method calls such as this one, Ruby manages to provide many useful function-like methods while keeping the core of the language relatively small and uncluttered.

This simple idea of dropping parentheses from method calls is used quite often by expert coders. Sometimes you'll want to keep the parentheses because they make a method's nature obvious—or maybe because the parser requires the parentheses to make sense of a complex line of code. Other times, you'll want to drop the parentheses to make the code cleaner or to make a method look like a keyword, as is the case with puts.

For another example of flexible syntax, think of object attributes, which are actually methods in disguise:

```
common_idioms/mimic_methods.rb
```

```ruby
class C
  def my_attribute=(value)
    @p = value
  end

  def my_attribute
    @p
  end
end

obj = C.new
obj.my_attribute = 'some value'
obj.my_attribute    # => "some value"
```

Writing obj.my_attribute = 'some value' is the same as writing obj.my_attribute=('some value'), but it looks cleaner.

What should we call disguised methods such as my_attribute and my_attribute=? Let's take a cue from zoology: an animal that disguises itself as another species is said to employ "mimicry." Following that pattern, a method call that disguises itself as something else, such as puts or obj.my_attribute=, can be called a *Mimic Method*.

Spell: Mimic Method, page 237

Mimic Methods are a very simple concept, but the more you look into Ruby, the more you find creative uses for them. For example, access modifiers such as private and protected are Mimic Methods, as are *Class Macros (117)* such as attr_reader. Popular libraries provide further examples. Here is one such example.

The Camping Example

The following snippet of code comes from an application written with the Camping web framework. It binds the /help URL to a specific controller action:

```ruby
class Help < R '/help'
    def get
      # rendering for HTTP GET...
```

Class Help seems to inherit from a class named R. But what's that quirky little string right after R? You might assume that Ruby would simply refuse this syntax, until you realize that R is actually a Mimic Method that takes a string and returns an instance of Class. That is the class that Help actually inherits from. (If the notion of a method returning a class sounds strange to you, consider that Ruby classes are just objects, as you can read in Chapter 2, *Monday: The Object Model*, on page 11.)

Thanks to creative tricks such as this one, Camping feels less like a Ruby web framework and more like a domain-specific language for web development. In general, this is a good thing, as I argue in Appendix 2, *Domain-Specific Languages*, on page 227.

Nil Guards

Most Ruby beginners looking through someone else's code are perplexed by this exotic idiom:

```
common_idioms/nil_guards.rb
a ||= []
```

In this example, the value to the right happens to be an empty array, but it could be any assignable value. The ||= is actually a syntax shortcut for the following:

```
a || (a = [])
```

To understand this code, you need to understand the details of the "or" operator (||). Superficially, the || operator simply returns true if either of the two operands is true—but there is some subtlety to this. Here's the way that || actually works.

Remember that in a Boolean operation, any value is considered true with the exception of nil and false. If the first operand is true, then || simply returns the first operand, and the second operand is never evaluated. If the first operand is *not* true, then || evaluates and returns the second operand instead. This means the result will be true unless both operands are false, which is consistent with the intuitive notion of an or operator.

Now you can see that the previous code has the same effect as this:

```
if defined?(a) && a
  a
else
  a = []
end
```

You can translate this code as this: "If a is nil, or false, or hasn't even been defined yet, then make it an empty array and give me its value; if it's anything else, just give me its value." In such cases, experienced Ruby coders generally consider the ||= operator more elegant and readable than an if. You're not limited to arrays, so you can use the same idiom to initialize just about anything. This idiom is sometimes called a *Nil Guard*, because it's used to make sure that a variable is not nil.

Spell: Nil Guard, page 238

Attribute Trouble

Object attributes (which I describe in *Mimic Methods*, on page 217) contain a hidden trap for the unsuspecting programmer:

common_idioms/attribute_trouble.rb

```ruby
class MyClass
  attr_accessor :my_attribute

  def set_attribute(n)
    my_attribute = n
  end
end

obj = MyClass.new
obj.set_attribute 10
obj.my_attribute          # => nil
```

This result is probably not what you expected. The problem is that the code in set_attribute is ambiguous. Ruby has no way of knowing whether this code is an assignment to a local variable called my_attribute or a call to a *Mimic Method (218)* called my_attribute=. When in doubt, Ruby defaults to the first option. It defines a variable called my_attribute, which immediately falls out of scope.

To steer clear of this problem, use self explicitly when you assign to an attribute of the current object. Continuing from the previous example:

```ruby
class MyClass
  def set_attribute(n)
➤   self.my_attribute = n
  end
end

obj.set_attribute 10
obj.my_attribute          # => 10
```

If you're a jaded Ruby expert, you might ask yourself a subtle question that completely escaped me while writing the first edition of this book. What if MyClass#my_attribute= happens to be private? In *What private Really Means*, on page 35, I said that you cannot call a private method with an explicit self receiver—so it seems that you're out of luck in this (exceedingly rare) case. The answer to this conundrum is one of Ruby's few ad-hoc exceptions. Attribute setters such as my_attribute= can be called with self even if they're private:

```ruby
class MyClass
  private :my_attribute=
end

obj.set_attribute 11      # No error!
obj.my_attribute          # => 11
```

Nil Guards are also used quite often to initialize instance variables. Look at this class:

```
class C
  def initialize
    @a = []
  end

  def elements
    @a
  end
end
```

By using a Nil Guard, you can rewrite the same code more succinctly:

```
class C
  def elements
    @a ||= []
  end
end
```

The previous code initializes the instance variable at the latest possible moment, when it's actually accessed. This idiom is called a *Lazy Instance Variable*. Sometimes, as in the earlier example, you manage to replace the whole initialize method with one or more Lazy Instance Variables.

Spell: Lazy Instance Variable, page 237

Nil Guards and Boolean Values

Nil Guards have one quirk that is worth mentioning: they don't work well with Boolean values. Here is an example:

```
def calculate_initial_value
  puts "called: calculate_initial_value"
  false
end

b = nil
2.times do
  b ||= calculate_initial_value
end
```

```
❮ called: calculate_initial_value
  called: calculate_initial_value
```

The Nil Guard in the code above doesn't seem to work—calculate_initial_value is called twice, instead of once as you might expect. To see where the problem is, let's write the if equivalent of that Nil Guard.

```
if defined?(b) && b
  # if b is already defined and neither nil nor false:
  b
else
  # if b is undefined, nil or false:
  b = calculate_initial_value
end
```

If you look at this if-based translation of a Nil Guard, you will see that Nil Guards are unable to distinguish false from nil. In our previous example, b is false, so the Nil Guard reinitializes it every time.

This little wrinkle of Nil Guards usually goes unnoticed, but it can also cause the occasional hard-to-spot bug. For this reason, you shouldn't use Nil Guards to initialize variables that can have false (or nil, for that matter) as a legitimate value.

Self Yield

When you pass a block to a method, you expect the method to call back to the block with yield. A twist on callbacks is that an object can also pass *itself* to the block. Let's see how this can be useful.

The Faraday Example

In the Faraday HTTP library, you typically initialize an HTTP connection with a URL and a block:

common_idioms/faraday_example.rb

```
require 'faraday'

conn = Faraday.new("https://twitter.com/search") do |faraday|
  faraday.response        :logger
  faraday.adapter         Faraday.default_adapter
  faraday.params["q"]   = "ruby"
  faraday.params["src"] = "typd"
end

response = conn.get
response.status              # => 200
```

This code sets the parameters for the connection. If you wish, you can get the same results by passing a hash of parameters to Faraday.new—but the block-based style has the advantage of making it clear that all the statements in the block are focusing on the same object. If you like this style, you might want to peek inside Faraday's source code and see how it is implemented. Faraday.new actually creates and returns a Faraday::Connection object:

gems/faraday-0.8.8/lib/faraday.rb

```
module Faraday
  class << self
    def new(url = nil, options = {})
      # ...
      Faraday::Connection.new(url, options, &block)
    end

    # ...
```

The interesting stuff happens in Faraday::Connection#initialize. This method accepts an optional block and yields the newly created Connection object to the block:

gems/faraday-0.8.8/lib/faraday/connection.rb

```
module Faraday
  class Connection
    def initialize(url = nil, options = {})
      # ...
      yield self if block_given?
      # ...
    end

    # ...
```

This simple idiom is known as a *Self Yield*. Self Yields are pretty common in Ruby—even instance_eval and class_eval optionally yield self to the block, although this feature is rarely used in practice:

Spell: Self Yield, page 241

common_idioms/self_yield_in_eval.rb

```
String.class_eval do |klass|
  klass # => String
end
```

For a more creative example of a Self Yield, you can check out the tap method.

The tap() Example

In Ruby, it's common to find long chains of method calls such as this:

common_idioms/tap.rb

```
['a', 'b', 'c'].push('d').shift.upcase.next # => "B"
```

Chains of calls are frowned upon in most languages (and sometimes referred to as "train wrecks"). Ruby's terse syntax makes call chains generally more readable, but they still present a problem: if you have an error somewhere along the chain, it can be difficult to track down the error.

For example, maybe you're worried that the call to shift is not returning what you expect. To confirm your suspicions, you break the chain and print out the result of shift (or set a breakpoint in your debugger):

```
temp = ['a', 'b', 'c'].push('d').shift
puts temp
x = temp.upcase.next
```

❮ a

This is a clumsy way to debug your code. If you don't want to split the call chain, you can use the tap method to slip intermediate operations into the middle of a call chain:

```
['a', 'b', 'c'].push('d').shift.tap {|x| puts x }.upcase.next
```

❮ a

The tap method already exists on Kernel. However, it's a good exercise to imagine how you would write it yourself if it weren't already provided by Ruby:

```
class Object
  def tap
    yield self
    self
  end
end
```

Symbol#to_proc()

This exotic spell is popular among black-belt Ruby programmers. When I stumbled upon this spell for the first time, I had trouble understanding the reasoning behind it. It's easier to get there by taking one small step at a time.

Look at this code:

common_idioms/symbol_to_proc.rb

```
names = ['bob', 'bill', 'heather']
names.map {|name| name.capitalize }    # => ["Bob", "Bill", "Heather"]
```

Focus on the block—a simple "one-call block" that takes a single argument and calls a single method on that argument. One-call blocks are very common in Ruby, especially (but not exclusively) when you're dealing with arrays.

In a language such as Ruby, which prides itself on being succinct and to the point, even a one-call block looks verbose. Why do you have to go through the trouble of creating a block, with curly braces and all, just to ask Ruby to call a method? The idea of Symbol#to_proc is that you can replace a one-call block with a shorter construct. Let's start with the smallest piece of information you need, which is the name of the method that you want to call, as a symbol:

```
:capitalize
```

You want to convert the symbol to a one-call block like this:

```
{|x| x.capitalize }
```

As a first step, you can add a method to the Symbol class, which converts the symbol to a Proc object:

```
class Symbol
  def to_proc
    Proc.new {|x| x.send(self) }
  end
end
```

See how this method works? If you call it on, say, the :capitalize symbol, it returns a proc that takes an argument and calls capitalize on the argument. Now you can use to_proc and the & modifier to convert a symbol to a Proc and then to a block:

```
names = ['bob', 'bill', 'heather']
names.map(&:capitalize.to_proc)    # => ["Bob", "Bill", "Heather"]
```

You can make this code even shorter. As it turns out, you can apply the & modifier to any object, and it will take care of converting that object to a Proc by calling to_proc. (You didn't think we picked the name of the to_proc method randomly, did you?) So, you can simply write the following:

```
names = ['bob', 'bill', 'heather']
names.map(&:capitalize)    # => ["Bob", "Bill", "Heather"]
```

That's the trick known as *Symbol To Proc*. Neat, huh?

Spell: Symbol To Proc, page 242

The good news is that you don't have to write Symbol#to_proc, because it's already provided by Ruby. In fact, Ruby's implementation of Symbol#to_proc also supports blocks with more than one argument, which are required by methods such as inject:

```
# without Symbol#to_proc:
[1, 2, 5].inject(0) {|memo, obj| memo + obj }    # => 8

# with Symbol#to_proc:
[1, 2, 5].inject(0, &:+)  # => 8

# cool!
```

Domain-Specific Languages

Domain-specific languages are a popular topic these days. They overlap somewhat with metaprogramming, so you'll probably want to know a thing or two about them.

The Case for Domain-Specific Languages

Are you old enough to remember *Zork*? It was one of the first "text adventures": text-based computer games that were popular in the early 1980s. Here are the first few lines from a game of *Zork*:

```
❮ West of house
  You are standing in an open field west of a
  white house, with a boarded front door.
  You see a small mailbox here.
⇒ open mailbox
❮ Opening the small mailbox reveals a leaflet.
⇒ take leaflet
❮ Taken.
```

Suppose you have to write a text adventure as your next job. What language would you write it in?

You'd probably pick a language that's good at manipulating strings and supports object-oriented programming. But whatever language you chose, you'd still have a gap between that language and the problem you're trying to solve. This probably happens in your daily programming job as well. For example, many large Java applications deal with money, but Money is not a standard Java type. That means each application has to reinvent money, usually as a class.

In the case of our adventure game, you have to deal with entities such as rooms and items. No general-purpose language supports these entities directly. How would you like a language that's specifically targeted to text adventures? Given such a language, you could write code like this:

```
me: Actor
    location = westOfHouse
;

westOfHouse : Room 'West of house'
    "You are standing in an open field west of
     a white house, with a boarded front door."
;

+ mailbox : OpenableContainer 'mailbox' 'small mailbox';

++ leaflet : Thing 'leaflet' 'leaflet';
```

This is not a mocked-up example—it's real code. It's written in a language called TADS, specifically designed for creating "interactive fiction" (today's fancier name for text adventures). TADS is an example of a *domain-specific language* (DSL), a language that focuses on a specific problem domain.

The opposite of a DSL is a *general-purpose language* (GPL), such as C++ or Ruby. You can use a GPL to tackle a wide variety of problems, even if it might be more suited to some problems than others. Whenever you write a program, it's up to you to choose between a flexible GPL and a focused DSL.

Let's assume that you decide to go down the DSL route. How would you proceed then?

Using DSLs

If you want a DSL for your own specific problem, you might get lucky. There are hundreds of DSLs around, focusing on a wide range of domains. The UNIX shell is a DSL for gluing command-line utilities together. Microsoft's VBA was designed to extend Excel and other Microsoft Office applications. The make language is a DSL focused on building C programs, and Ant is an XML-based equivalent of make for Java programs. Some of these languages are limited in scope, while others are flexible enough to cross the line into GPL-dom.

What if you can't find a ready-made DSL that fits the domain you're working in? In that case, you can write your own DSL and then use that DSL to write your program. You could say that this process—writing a DSL and then using it—is another take on metaprogramming. It can be a slippery path, though. You'll probably need to define a grammar for your language with a system such as ANTLR or Yacc, which are themselves DSLs for writing language parsers. As the scope of your problem expands, your humble little language can grow into a GPL before you even realize it. At that point, your leisurely foray into language writing will have escalated into an exhausting marathon.

To avoid these difficulties, you can pick a different route. Rather than writing a full-fledged DSL, you can bend a GPL into something resembling a DSL for your specific problem. The next section shows you how.

Internal and External DSLs

Let's see an example of a DSL that's actually a GPL in disguise. Here's a snippet of Ruby code that uses the Markaby gem to generate HTML:

dsl/markaby_example.rb

```
require 'markaby'

html = Markaby::Builder.new do
  head { title "My wonderful home page" }
  body do
    h1 "Welcome to my home page!"
    b "My hobbies:"
    ul do
      li "Juggling"
      li "Knitting"
      li "Metaprogramming"
    end
  end
end
```

This code is plain old Ruby, but it looks like a specific language for HTML generation. You can call Markaby an *internal DSL*, because it lives within a larger, general-purpose language. By contrast, languages that have their own parser, such as make, are often called *external DSLs*. One example of an external DSL is the Ant build language. Even though the Ant interpreter is written in Java, the Ant language is completely different from Java.

Let's leave the GPL vs. DSL match behind us and assume that you want to use a DSL. Which DSL should you prefer? An internal DSL or an external DSL?

One advantage of an internal DSL is that you can easily fall back on the underlying GPL whenever you need to do so. However, the syntax of your internal DSL will be constrained by the syntax of the GPL behind it. This is a big problem with some languages. For example, you can write an internal DSL in Java, but the result is probably still going to look pretty much like Java. But with Ruby, you can write an internal DSL that looks more like an *ad hoc* language tailored to the problem at hand. Thanks to Ruby's flexible, uncluttered syntax, the Markaby example shown earlier barely looks like Ruby at all.

That's why Ruby programmers tend to use Ruby where Java programmers would use an external language or an XML file. It's easier to adapt Ruby to your own needs than it is to adapt Java. As an example, consider build languages. The standard build languages for Java and C (Ant and make, respectively) are external DSLs, while the standard build language for Ruby (Rake) is just a Ruby library—an internal DSL.

DSLs and Metaprogramming

At the beginning of this book, we defined metaprogramming as "writing code that writes code" (or, if you want to be more precise, "writing code that manipulates the language constructs at runtime"). Now that you know about DSLs, you have another definition of metaprogramming: "designing a domain-specific language and then using that DSL to write your program."

This is a book about the first definition, not a book about DSLs. To write a DSL, you have to deal with a number of challenges that are outside the scope of this book. You have to understand your domain, care about your language's user-friendliness, and carefully evaluate the constraints and tradeoffs of your grammar. While writing this book, I opted to keep this particular can of worms shut.

Still, metaprogramming and DSLs have a close relationship in the Ruby world. To build an internal DSL, you must bend the language itself, and doing so requires many of the techniques described in this book. Put another way, metaprogramming provides the bricks that you need to build DSLs. If you're interested in internal Ruby DSLs, this book contains information that's important for you.

Whenever someone says they have "a cool trick," take them outside
and slap them up.

> *Jim Weirich (1956–2014)*

Spell Book

This appendix is a "spell book"—a quick reference to all the "spells" in the book, in alphabetical order. Most of these spells are metaprogramming related (but the ones from Appendix 1, *Common Idioms*, on page 217, are arguably not that "meta"). Each spell comes with a short example and a reference to the page where it's introduced. Go to the associated pages for extended examples and the reasoning behind each spell.

The Spells

Around Alias

Call the previous, aliased version of a method from a redefined method.

```ruby
class String
  alias_method :old_reverse, :reverse

  def reverse
    "x#{old_reverse}x"
  end
end

"abc".reverse # => "xcbax"
```

For more information, see page 134.

Blank Slate

Remove methods from an object to turn them into *Ghost Methods (57)*.

```ruby
class C
  def method_missing(name, *args)
    "a Ghost Method"
  end
end
```

```ruby
obj = C.new
obj.to_s # => "#<C:0x007fbb2a10d2f8>"

class D < BasicObject
  def method_missing(name, *args)
    "a Ghost Method"
  end
end

blank_slate = D.new
blank_slate.to_s # => "a Ghost Method"
```

For more information, see page 66.

Class Extension

Define class methods by mixing a module into a class's singleton class (a special case of *Object Extension (130)*).

```ruby
class C; end

module M
  def my_method
    'a class method'
  end
end

class << C
  include M
end

C.my_method # => "a class method"
```

For more information, see page 130.

Class Instance Variable

Store class-level state in an instance variable of the Class object.

```ruby
class C
  @my_class_instance_variable = "some value"

  def self.class_attribute
    @my_class_instance_variable
  end
end

C.class_attribute # => "some value"
```

For more information, see page 110.

Class Macro

Use a class method in a class definition.

```
class C; end

class << C
  def my_macro(arg)
    "my_macro(#{arg}) called"
  end
end

class C
  my_macro :x # => "my_macro(x) called"
end
```

For more information, see page 117.

Clean Room

Use an object as an environment in which to evaluate a block.

```
class CleanRoom
  def a_useful_method(x); x * 2; end
end

CleanRoom.new.instance_eval { a_useful_method(3) }    # => 6
```

For more information, see page 87.

Code Processor

Process *Strings of Code (141)* from an external source.

```
File.readlines("a_file_containing_lines_of_ruby.txt").each do |line|
  puts "#{line.chomp} ==> #{eval(line)}"
end

# >> 1 + 1 ==> 2
# >> 3 * 2 ==> 6
# >> Math.log10(100) ==> 2.0
```

For more information, see page 144.

Context Probe

Execute a block to access information in an object's context.

```ruby
class C
  def initialize
    @x = "a private instance variable"
  end
end

obj = C.new
obj.instance_eval { @x } # => "a private instance variable"
```

For more information, see page 85.

Deferred Evaluation

Store a piece of code and its context in a proc or lambda for evaluation later.

```ruby
class C
  def store(&block)
    @my_code_capsule = block
  end

  def execute
    @my_code_capsule.call
  end
end

obj = C.new
obj.store { $X = 1 }
$X = 0

obj.execute
$X # => 1
```

For more information, see page 89.

Dynamic Dispatch

Decide which method to call at runtime.

```ruby
method_to_call = :reverse
obj = "abc"

obj.send(method_to_call) # => "cba"
```

For more information, see page 48.

Dynamic Method

Decide how to define a method at runtime.

```
class C
end

C.class_eval do
  define_method :my_method do
    "a dynamic method"
  end
end

obj = C.new
obj.my_method # => "a dynamic method"
```

For more information, see page 51.

Dynamic Proxy

Dynamically forward method calls to another object.

```
class MyDynamicProxy
  def initialize(target)
    @target = target
  end

  def method_missing(name, *args, &block)
    "result: #{@target.send(name, *args, &block)}"
  end
end

obj = MyDynamicProxy.new("a string")
obj.reverse # => "result: gnirts a"
```

For more information, see page 60.

Flat Scope

Use a closure to share variables between two scopes.

```
class C
  def an_attribute
    @attr
  end
end

obj = C.new
a_variable = 100

# flat scope:
obj.instance_eval do
  @attr = a_variable
end
```

```
obj.an_attribute # => 100
```

For more information, see page 83.

Ghost Method

Respond to a message that doesn't have an associated method.

```
class C
  def method_missing(name, *args)
    name.to_s.reverse
  end
end

obj = C.new
obj.my_ghost_method # => "dohtem_tsohg_ym"
```

For more information, see page 57.

Hook Method

Override a method to intercept object model events.

```
$INHERITORS = []
class C
  def self.inherited(subclass)
    $INHERITORS << subclass
  end
end

class D < C
end

class E < C
end

class F < E
end

$INHERITORS # => [D, E, F]
```

For more information, see page 157.

Kernel Method

Define a method in module Kernel to make the method available to all objects.

```ruby
module Kernel
  def a_method
    "a kernel method"
  end
end

a_method # => "a kernel method"
```

For more information, see page 32.

Lazy Instance Variable

Wait until the first access to initialize an instance variable.

```ruby
class C
  def attribute
    @attribute = @attribute || "some value"
  end
end

obj = C.new
obj.attribute # => "some value"
```

For more information, see page 221.

Mimic Method

Disguise a method as another language construct.

```ruby
def BaseClass(name)
  name == "string" ? String : Object
end

class C < BaseClass "string"  # a method that looks like a class
  attr_accessor :an_attribute  # a method that looks like a keyword
end

obj = C.new
obj.an_attribute = 1   # a method that looks like an attribute
```

For more information, see page 218.

Monkeypatch

Change the features of an existing class.

```
"abc".reverse # => "cba"

class String
  def reverse
    "override"
  end
end

"abc".reverse # => "override"
```

For more information, see page 16.

Namespace

Define constants within a module to avoid name clashes.

```
module MyNamespace
  class Array
    def to_s
      "my class"
    end
  end
end

Array.new # => []
MyNamespace::Array.new # => my class
```

For more information, see page 23.

Nil Guard

Override a reference to nil with an "or."

```
x = nil
y = x || "a value" # => "a value"
```

For more information, see page 219.

Object Extension

Define Singleton Methods by mixing a module into an object's singleton class.

```ruby
obj = Object.new

module M
  def my_method
    'a singleton method'
  end
end

class << obj
  include M
end

obj.my_method # => "a singleton method"
```

For more information, see page 130.

Open Class

Modify an existing class.

```ruby
class String
  def my_string_method
    "my method"
  end
end

"abc".my_string_method # => "my method"
```

For more information, see page 14.

Prepended Wrapper

Call a method from its prepended override.

```ruby
module M
  def reverse
    "x#{super}x"
  end
end

String.class_eval do
  prepend M
end

"abc".reverse # => "xcbax"
```

For more information, see page 136.

Refinement

Patch a class until the end of the file, or until the end of the including module.

```
module MyRefinement
  refine String do
    def reverse
      "my reverse"
    end
  end
end

"abc".reverse # => "cba"
using MyRefinement
"abc".reverse # => "my reverse"
```

For more information, see page 36.

Refinement Wrapper

Call an unrefined method from its refinement.

```
module StringRefinement
  refine String do
    def reverse
      "x#{super}x"
    end
  end
end

using StringRefinement
"abc".reverse # => "xcbax"
```

For more information, see page 135.

Sandbox

Execute untrusted code in a safe environment.

```
def sandbox(&code)
  proc {
    $SAFE = 2
    yield
  }.call
end
begin
  sandbox { File.delete 'a_file' }
rescue Exception => ex
  ex   # => #<SecurityError: Insecure operation at level 2>
end
```

For more information, see page 149.

Scope Gate

Isolate a scope with the class, module, or def keyword.

```
a = 1
defined? a # => "local-variable"

module MyModule
  b = 1
  defined? a # => nil
  defined? b # => "local-variable"
end

defined? a  # => "local-variable"
defined? b  # => nil
```

For more information, see page 81.

Self Yield

Pass self to the current block.

```
class Person
  attr_accessor :name, :surname

  def initialize
    yield self
  end
end

joe = Person.new do |p|
  p.name = 'Joe'
  p.surname = 'Smith'
end
```

For more information, see page 223.

Shared Scope

Share variables among multiple contexts in the same *Flat Scope (83)*.

```
lambda {
  shared = 10
  self.class.class_eval do
    define_method :counter do
      shared
    end
    define_method :down do
      shared -= 1
    end
  end
}.call

counter           # => 10
3.times { down }
counter           # => 7
```

For more information, see page 84.

Singleton Method

Define a method on a single object.

```ruby
obj = "abc"

class << obj
  def my_singleton_method
    "x"
  end
end

obj.my_singleton_method # => "x"
```

For more information, see page 115.

String of Code

Evaluate a string of Ruby code.

```ruby
my_string_of_code = "1 + 1"
eval(my_string_of_code) # => 2
```

For more information, see page 141.

Symbol To Proc

Convert a symbol to a block that calls a single method.

```ruby
[1, 2, 3, 4].map(&:even?)   # => [false, true, false, true]
```

For more information, see page 225.

Index

Advanced Rails and Node the Right Way

What used to be the realm of experts is fast becoming the stuff of day-to-day development—jump to the head of the class in Ruby on Rails, and see how to do Node the right way.

Crafting Rails 4 Applications

Get ready to see Rails as you've never seen it before. Learn how to extend the framework, change its behavior, and replace whole components to bend it to your will. Eight different test-driven tutorials will help you understand Rails' inner workings and prepare you to tackle complicated projects with solutions that are well-tested, modular, and easy to maintain.

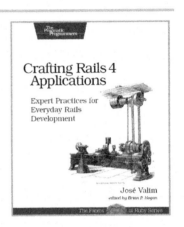

This second edition of the bestselling *Crafting Rails Applications* has been updated to Rails 4 and discusses new topics such as streaming, mountable engines, and thread safety.

José Valim
(208 pages) ISBN: 9781937785550. $36
https://pragprog.com/book/jvrails2

Node.js the Right Way

Get to the forefront of server-side JavaScript programming by writing compact, robust, fast, networked Node applications that scale. Ready to take JavaScript beyond the browser, explore dynamic languages features and embrace evented programming? Explore the fun, growing repository of Node modules provided by npm. Work with multiple protocols, load-balanced RESTful web services, express, ØMQ, Redis, CouchDB, and more. Develop production-grade Node applications fast.

Jim R. Wilson
(148 pages) ISBN: 9781937785734. $17
https://pragprog.com/book/jwnode

Put the "Fun" in Functional

Elixir puts the "fun" back into functional programming, on top of the robust, battle-tested, industrial-strength environment of Erlang.

Programming Elixir 1.2

You want to explore functional programming, but are put off by the academic feel (tell me about monads just one more time). You know you need concurrent applications, but also know these are almost impossible to get right. Meet Elixir, a functional, concurrent language built on the rock-solid Erlang VM. Elixir's pragmatic syntax and built-in support for metaprogramming will make you productive and keep you interested for the long haul. This book is *the* introduction to Elixir for experienced programmers.

Maybe you need something that's closer to Ruby, but with a battle-proven environment that's unrivaled for massive scalability, concurrency, distribution, and fault tolerance. Maybe the time is right for the Next Big Thing. Maybe it's *Elixir*.

This edition of the book has been updated to cover Elixir 1.2, including the new with expression, the exrm release manager, and the removal of deprecated types.

Dave Thomas
(354 pages) ISBN: 9781680501667. $38
https://pragprog.com/book/elixir12

Programming Erlang (2nd edition)

A multi-user game, web site, cloud application, or networked database can have thousands of users all interacting at the same time. You need a powerful, industrial-strength tool to handle the really hard problems inherent in parallel, concurrent environments. You need Erlang. In this second edition of the bestselling *Programming Erlang*, you'll learn how to write parallel programs that scale effortlessly on multicore systems.

Joe Armstrong
(548 pages) ISBN: 9781937785536. $42
https://pragprog.com/book/jaerlang2

What You Need to Know

Each new version of the Web brings its own gold rush. Here are your tools.

HTML5 and CSS3 (2nd edition)

HTML5 and CSS3 are more than just buzzwords—they're the foundation for today's web applications. This book gets you up to speed on the HTML5 elements and CSS3 features you can use right now in your current projects, with backwards compatible solutions that ensure that you don't leave users of older browsers behind. This new edition covers even more new features, including CSS animations, IndexedDB, and client-side validations.

Brian P. Hogan
(314 pages) ISBN: 9781937785598. $38
https://pragprog.com/book/bhh52e

Web Development Recipes 2nd Edition

Modern web development is so much more than just HTML and CSS with a little JavaScript mixed in. People want faster, more usable interfaces that work on multiple devices, and you need the latest tools and techniques to make that happen. This book gives you over 40 concise solutions to today's web development problems, and introduces new solutions that will expand your skill set – proven, practical advice from authors who use these tools and techniques every day. In this completely updated edition, you'll find innovative new techniques and workflows, as well as reworked solutions that take advantage of new developments.

Brian P. Hogan, Chris Warren, Mike Weber, and Chris Johnson
(358 pages) ISBN: 9781680500561. $38
https://pragprog.com/book/wbdev2

Explore Testing and Cucumber

Explore the uncharted waters of exploratory testing and delve deeper into Cucumber.

Explore It!

Uncover surprises, risks, and potentially serious bugs with exploratory testing. Rather than designing all tests in advance, explorers design and execute small, rapid experiments, using what they learned from the last little experiment to inform the next. Learn essential skills of a master explorer, including how to analyze software to discover key points of vulnerability, how to design experiments on the fly, how to hone your observation skills, and how to focus your efforts.

Elisabeth Hendrickson
(186 pages) ISBN: 9781937785024. $29
https://pragprog.com/book/ehxta

The Cucumber Book

Your customers want rock-solid, bug-free software that does exactly what they expect it to do. Yet they can't always articulate their ideas clearly enough for you to turn them into code. *The Cucumber Book* dives straight into the core of the problem: communication between people. Cucumber saves the day; it's a testing, communication, and requirements tool – all rolled into one.

Matt Wynne and Aslak Hellesøy
(336 pages) ISBN: 9781934356807. $30
https://pragprog.com/book/hwcuc

The Pragmatic Bookshelf

The Pragmatic Bookshelf features books written by developers for developers. The titles continue the well-known Pragmatic Programmer style and continue to garner awards and rave reviews. As development gets more and more difficult, the Pragmatic Programmers will be there with more titles and products to help you stay on top of your game.

Visit Us Online

This Book's Home Page
https://pragprog.com/book/ppmetr2
Source code from this book, errata, and other resources. Come give us feedback, too!

Register for Updates
https://pragprog.com/updates
Be notified when updates and new books become available.

Join the Community
https://pragprog.com/community
Read our weblogs, join our online discussions, participate in our mailing list, interact with our wiki, and benefit from the experience of other Pragmatic Programmers.

New and Noteworthy
https://pragprog.com/news
Check out the latest pragmatic developments, new titles and other offerings.

Save on the eBook

Save on the eBook versions of this title. Owning the paper version of this book entitles you to purchase the electronic versions at a terrific discount.

PDFs are great for carrying around on your laptop—they are hyperlinked, have color, and are fully searchable. Most titles are also available for the iPhone and iPod touch, Amazon Kindle, and other popular e-book readers.

Buy now at *https://pragprog.com/coupon*

Contact Us

Online Orders:	*https://pragprog.com/catalog*
Customer Service:	*support@pragprog.com*
International Rights:	*translations@pragprog.com*
Academic Use:	*academic@pragprog.com*
Write for Us:	*http://write-for-us.pragprog.com*
Or Call:	+1 800-699-7764

CPSIA information can be obtained at www.ICGtesting.com
Printed in the USA
BVOW09s1423191016

465447BV00005B/70/P